Arguing Religion

A Bishop Speaks at **Facebook** and **Google** ⌕

Word on Fire, Park Ridge, IL 60068
© 2018 by Word on Fire Catholic Ministries
Printed in the United States of America

21 20   3 4
ISBN: 978-1-943-24337-2

Library of Congress Control Number: 2018956828
Barron, Robert E., 1959-

www.wordonfire.org

CONTENTS

Introduction
SPEAKING AT FACEBOOK AND GOOGLE

i

Section One
HOW TO HAVE A RELIGIOUS ARGUMENT

1

Faith Is Not Opposed to Reason — 6

Overcoming Scientism — 17

Be Intolerant of Toleration — 27

Avoid Voluntarism — 37

Seek to Understand Your Opponent's Position — 46

Follow the Example of Thomas Aquinas — 51

Section Two
RELIGION AND THE OPENING UP OF THE MIND

59

An Argument for God's Existence — 66

Elijah and the Priests of Ba'al — 81

The Burning Bush — 100

Conclusion

107

Notes

113

Introduction

SPEAKING AT FACEBOOK AND GOOGLE

EARLY IN 2017, I received a visit from five gentlemen from San Jose, California. Though we had never met before, they had been following my work for some time. They told me that they were all, in various capacities, involved in the culture of Silicon Valley and that they wanted to find a way to introduce me to that highly-influential world, perhaps by setting up speaking engagements for me at the headquarters of Facebook and Google. I responded positively and we all shook hands, but I must admit that I didn't think their plan would come to much. About six months later, to my delight and surprise, one of these men called me to say that a representative from a "Catholic group" at Facebook would be contacting me shortly to schedule a talk at their headquarters in Menlo Park, California.

The Facebook compound is a fascinating place: cutting edge architecture, open work zones for the employees, a giant cafeteria to rival the dining areas at major universities, bicycles everywhere, a garden for meditating and strolling on the roof of one of the principal buildings, and, above all, young people. I don't know if I saw one denizen of Facebook over thirty. I felt more or less like Methuselah.

But I was very warmly received, as an enthusiastic crowd attended my lecture. The talk was also live-streamed to thousands of viewers worldwide, and as I write this, the video has nearly 500,000 views. The topic I spoke on was "How to Have a Religious Argument." I decided not to address any particular theological theme in an apologetic manner, but rather to step back and consider how we might begin to approach the discussion of religious issues. I have long endorsed Stanley Hauerwas' claim that one of the most pressing demands of our violent and volatile time is to learn again how to have a religious argument in public. From fairly extensive experience on Facebook and other social media websites, I know that people are quite adept when it comes to shouting about religion, but that very few know how to constructively, rationally, and helpfully enter into conversation about religious matters.

About six weeks after the Facebook presentation, I was contacted, again through the kindly ministrations of my friends from San Jose, by a representative of Catholics who work at Google. They proposed the same sort of arrangement, and I happily acquiesced. Like Facebook's headquarters, the Google campus looked like the kind of world that millennials would build if you gave them infinite amounts of money: lots of open space, a gym, napping pods in the work areas, music rooms, etc. I will confess that, as I explored both facilities, I often smiled, wondering what my no-nonsense, Greatest-Generation father would have made of all of it. But then I reminded myself that I was touring the workplaces of arguably the most successful, culture-influencing operations on the planet. So if napping and bike-riding help, more power to them.

For the talk at Google, I decided to broach the topic of religion more directly, taking as my cue the idea, dear to all Google-users, of the search. I titled the talk "Religion and the Opening Up of the Mind." Religion, I argued, is born of the human being's essentially unlimited capacity to quest, both intellectually and spiritually. Far from shutting down the mind—as is so often claimed by its critics—religion expands the mind and pushes it ever further, toward a properly infinite goal.

The book you are reading is a slightly expanded version of the lectures I gave at Facebook and Google.

The intended audience is not so much the convinced religious believer, but rather the outsider, the seeker, the skeptic. The tone that I adopted for both lectures is rather elevated intellectually. This is because I'm convinced that a dumbed-down religion, practiced across the denominational divides for about the past fifty years, has been a disaster. When the "new atheist" critiques arose fifteen years ago, most believers in God didn't have a clue how to respond to what were, basically, tired arguments and crude caricatures. Especially in our increasingly secularized culture, we need a smart presentation of faith.

My hope is that this little book might find its way into the hands of those, especially the young, who have wandered from God. May it be an invitation to take another look, and perhaps even to come home.

Section One

HOW TO HAVE
A RELIGIOUS ARGUMENT

I F YOU HAVE the slightest acquaintance with the internet, you know that people in the digital space fight about religious matters all the time. The comment boxes of religious and atheist sites are among the most visited and most heated in the virtual world. I know this not only from my perusal of such sites, but also from nearly twenty years of direct experience running websites and social media connected to my Word on Fire ministry. When I posted my first YouTube videos, I was frankly surprised to see that people could comment on my offerings. I was barely over my surprise when I became appalled at the content of the commentary. Around 90 percent of the posted reactions were sharply negative, arising from people who hated God, religion, and me, roughly in that order.

What has become abundantly clear to me over the years is that, though there is a great deal of energy around matters religious, and though lots of sharp words are regularly exchanged, very few of the people on the internet really know how to have an *argument* about religion. They don't know, at least in regard to matters religious, how to marshal evidence, construct syllogisms, draw valid conclusions, listen and respond to objections, etc. Much of this incapacity is a function of an assumption that is operative in both the high and the low culture—namely, that when it comes to religion, there are only two lively options: either aggressive, even violent imposition of one's views, or a bland and universal toleration of all opinions. And underneath that assumption is the even more fundamental conviction that religion is finally irrational, a matter of complexes and fantasies rather than reason. What I want strenuously to advocate for our time is a *tertium quid*, a third way that was taken for granted for large swaths of Western history: real argument about religion. I want to be clear at the very outset that in calling for argument, I'm not encouraging religious conflict. Just the contrary! The more we cultivate rational speech around matters religious, the more peaceful our increasingly roiled culture will be.

In the course of this section, I will endeavor to lay out five conditions or prerequisites for the formulation of this sort of argument. I trust it will become clear that these are as much behavioral and attitudinal as strictly intellectual. Just as the disputants in a Platonic dialogue had to be schooled in an entire way of life before they were capable of entering into constructive conversation, so the restless men and women of our culture, conditioned by materialism, relativism, and the prerogative of self-assertion, must be habituated to a certain manner of being in the world before they can speak to one another fruitfully about matters of faith. They must come to understand—and put into practice—the convictions that authentic faith is not opposed to reason; that scientism must be put to rest; that mere toleration must not be tolerated; that voluntarism must be eschewed; and that opponents must seek to really listen to one another. As an exemplar of these various intellectual and moral virtues, I shall propose St. Thomas Aquinas, whose method of engaging religious questions is an optimal one for us today.

CHAPTER ONE

Faith Is Not Opposed to Reason

A COUPLE OF YEARS AGO, I was watching Bill Maher's program "Real Time." I'll admit that Maher for me is something of a guilty pleasure. Though he is one of the most virulent opponents of religion on the scene today, I'm drawn to his show, perhaps under the rubric of knowing one's enemies. This particular program featured a one-on-one interview with Ralph Reed, the well-known political activist and evangelical Christian. After bantering for five minutes or so on a number of political issues, Maher paused and said, "Now Ralph, you're a person of faith." Reed did not disagree. Then Maher said, "And this means that you accept all sorts of things on the basis of no evidence whatsoever." To my astonishment and chagrin, Reed simply responded, "Yes." I nearly threw my remote at the television screen. I have spent a good deal of my adult life fighting against just the sort of irrational fideism that Reed was apparently advocating. One of the signal graces of my life occurred when I was a high school freshman and heard the first of Aquinas' famous arguments for God's existence. From that moment on, I intuited that faith and reason are not opposed to one another but that they are, in point of fact, mutually implicative. A particular sadness of our time is that far too many people, both believers and nonbelievers, hold to some form of fideism. The former find themselves unwilling and unable to sustain a conversation with the wider culture, and the latter slough off religion, so conceived, as primitive and irrational.

Accordingly, an indispensable step toward making a coherent argument about religion is the clarification of the nature of faith. If Ralph Reed is right, then religious people can assert, emote about, or impose their belief, but they cannot argue about it. But authentic faith is not, in fact, infrarational; it is suprarational. The infrarational—what lies below reason—is the stuff of credulity, superstition, naiveté, or just plain stupidity, and no self-respecting adult should be the least bit interested in fostering or embracing it. It is quite properly shunned by mature religious people as it is by scientists and philosophers. The suprarational, on the other hand, is what lies beyond reason but never stands in contradiction to reason. It is indeed a type of knowing, but one that surpasses the ordinary powers of observation, experimentation, hypothesis formation, or rational reflection.

In order to make this a bit clearer, permit me to offer an analogy. Coming to know another human being well is always a function of, broadly speaking, reason and faith. If I am interested in someone, intrigued by her, I can discover an awful lot through the exercise of my own powers of investigation and ratiocination. I can observe her in different situations; I can read what she has written or analyze the details of a project that she has supervised; I can speak to her friends and enemies and get their impressions of her; I can do a Google search on her or read her Wikipedia page. And once I've actually met her, my reason continues to operate alertly as I assess what I'm learning and draw my own conclusions about her personality and motivations. Moreover, I continue to check my own experience of her against what I've already taken in, searching out points of confluence and contrast. All of this active engagement is productive and illuminating.

But if I want to know her heart, I have to stop investigating and start listening. Supposing that our friendship has grown sufficiently intense, she will, at a point of her own choosing, speak something of herself that I could never have known through my own efforts. She will reveal truths about her life, her motivations, her longings, her most intense inner experiences. And at this point, I will be compelled to make a decision whether or not I believe her. What would motivate this act of the will? I might reason that nothing she told me is fundamentally at odds with what I've come to know about her on my own, that it is, in fact, deeply congruent with the results of my own investigations. I might determine that it fits in with her general character and pattern of life. But most of all, I will accept what she has told me about herself because I've come to *trust* her. I will never be able fully to verify what she has revealed, but in accepting it (because I accept *her*), I come to a knowledge and appreciation of her that I could never have achieved any other way. My faith in her word is a risk, to be sure, but a deeply rewarding one. Now, once I've chosen to believe what I've been told, does my reason go to sleep? Of course not! I ruminate on what she has said, seek to understand it more completely, compare and contrast it with other truths I've garnered from interacting with her, etc. At no point in this process have I succumbed to irrationality. No move of my mind or will could be reasonably characterized as superstitious or credulous, and my rationality has never been negated. But its limits have been acknowledged and its tendency toward pride and epistemic tyranny has been resisted.

This is a very precise analogy to the play between reason and faith in matters religious. From ancient times, human beings have used their minds to understand truths about God, and they have, in point of fact, been remarkably successful. Plato, Aristotle, Cicero, Augustine, Anselm, Thomas Aquinas, Descartes, Leibniz, Whitehead, and many others have proposed compelling arguments for God's existence. In the second section of this book, we will examine one of these in some detail. Furthermore, on the basis of these demonstrations, philosophers have drawn conclusions about many of God's attributes, including his perfection, goodness, infinity, omnipotence, etc. St. Paul expressed his own confidence in this "natural" or rational theology when he said, in his letter to the Romans: "Ever since the creation of the world his eternal power and divine nature, invisible though they are, have been understood and seen through the things he has made." Aquinas referred to these insights garnered by reason as *preambula fidei* (preambles to the faith). Some people, he thought, gifted with sharp minds and sufficient leisure time, could enter into the forecourts of faith, as it were, discerning a number of fundamental truths about God and the things of God. He also spoke of this kind of natural theologizing, charmingly, as a *manuductio* (a leading by the hand). Just as we might take a young child by the hand and cajole him to walk, so the philosopher can lead the fallen and finite mind toward the consideration of the deeper and more intimate truths of revelation.

The claim of the great Abrahamic religions—and something that sets them apart from the religions and mysticisms of the East—is that God has spoken (*Deus dixit*). God is not a mere force or ontological principle dumbly present as the deep background of existence, nor has God remained sequestered in complete and indifferent transcendence. Rather, he has spoken personally to his people. Please don't think I'm talking literally about a booming voice echoing from the clouds. That image is a classic metaphor for what I'm describing. Rather, through the prophets, patriarchs, events, and institutions of Israel, God disclosed his heart to his people Israel. He communicated his passion, anger, tender mercy, and covenant fidelity. Then, in the fullness of time, he spoke, as the author of the letter to the Hebrews has it, "by a Son." The Word, which made the universe and filled the minds and mouths of the prophets, came finally in person, speaking the compassion that God is. "God is love, and those who abide in love abide in God, and God abides in them."

Now, in the face of this communication, one has a choice to make: belief or unbelief. No one is asking a prospective believer to abandon her reason or jettison the insights that she has arrived at through her own assessment of evidence and rational speculation. No one is expecting her to sink to the level of mere credulity. But she is indeed being asked whether she is willing to believe the person who has disclosed a truth that she cannot control and that she would never have arrived at unaided. She is asked whether she is willing to trust. It is fascinating to note how often the word *pistis* occurs in the pages of the New Testament. Usually translated as "faith," it does indeed carry the connotation of explicitly religious belief, but in a more basic sense, it means "trust." In his inaugural address in the Gospel of Mark, Jesus says, "The kingdom of God has come near; repent, and believe (*pisteuete*) in the good news." After calming the storm at sea, the Lord says to his frightened disciples, "Why are you afraid? Have you still no faith (*pistis*)?" After curing the blind man, Bartimaeus, Jesus blithely tells him, "Go; your faith (*pistis*) has made you well." In the great Last Supper discourse in the Gospel of John, the Lord tells his Apostles, "Believe in God, believe also in me." He is saying, in all these cases: "Have the courage to trust in me and in what I am telling and showing you. The life-changing, storm-calming, sight-restoring, purpose-giving truth that I embody is on offer. Are you willing to accept it?"

Now, let us suppose that someone makes the act of faith. His reason is not suppressed, no *sacrificium intellectus* (sacrifice of the intellect) is required. For critical intelligence takes in what faith has accepted, turns it over, analyzes it, meditates upon it, and draws conclusions from it. This process goes by the technical name of theology, and it was succinctly characterized by St. Anselm of Canterbury as *fides quaerens intellectum* (faith seeking understanding). Do you see now why describing faith as "accepting things on the basis of no evidence" is just silly? It's really as silly as saying that falling in love is superstitious.

John Henry Newman, the greatest Catholic theologian to have written in the English language, spent a lifetime wrestling with this issue of faith and reason. He was on the frontlines when powerful rationalistic critics of Christianity emerged in the nineteenth century. Newman took the intriguing tack of remarking how so much of our ordinary knowing is a function of both rational and non-rational moves. He observed that we very typically give complete assent to propositions for which there is far from clinching inferential support. To cite his famous example, we assent to the claim that England is an island without hesitation, though we cannot produce an airtight syllogistic argument to that effect. Rather, the surety of our knowledge is the result of a whole congeries of experiences, testimonies, hunches, conversations, empirical observations, historical witnesses, etc., none of which in itself is perfectly convincing, but all of which, taken together and converging on the same point, push the mind to assent. Similarly, a man's conviction that he will marry a particular woman is hardly the result of a rational demonstration; rather, it is the fruit of a long process of assessment—both rational and non-rational, both reasonable and beyond reason—of a range of evidences.

Thus, the religious person will accept the claim that God is love, but he won't be able to justify that acceptance in any straightforwardly philosophical manner. Instead, if he reflects upon his assent, he will recognize in it elements of both reason and trust. Newman's point is that, in this, religious assent is not qualitatively different from ordinary acts of assent, even regarding the simplest matters. And this is why he can say, in one of his sermons on faith and reason, that "faith is the reasoning of a religious mind."

In the great temple of Jerusalem there were precincts reserved only for Jewish believers, but there was also a section called "the courtyard of the Gentiles." There, nonbelievers could gather and garner some sense of the holiness of the place. I fully realize that there are an awful lot of people today who have rejected religion, who are angry at religious institutions, or who have bought into the atheist critics of faith. I certainly don't expect such people to come right into the temple with eagerness and enthusiasm. But I wonder whether I might invite them into the courtyard of the Gentiles—which is to say, the arena of what I've characterized as natural theology or philosophical reflection on the things of God. I am not asking them to leave their brains at the door. On the contrary, I want them to pose any and all relevant questions. I would propose as common ground only the epistemic imperatives formulated by the twentieth-century Jesuit philosopher Bernard Lonergan: be attentive, be intelligent, be reasonable, and be responsible. Trust me, we will have a great deal to talk about.

CHAPTER TWO

Overcoming Scientism

ASECOND MAJOR BLOCK to mounting a real argument about matters religious is scientism, which I would define as the reduction of all knowledge to the scientific form of knowledge. This epistemological reductionism is rampant today, especially among younger people, and it is easy enough to see why. The manner of knowing born of the scientific method—observe, measure, hypothesize, experiment, draw conclusions, verify those conclusions through repeated experiment—has proven massively successful. Whereas more abstract, philosophical truths are quite difficult to test in practice, scientific claims can be readily confirmed or negated. Moreover, the technologies that have followed upon scientific advances are immediately useful to people all over the world, providing health, comfort, and entertainment.

The obvious success of this approach has led many to conclude that knowing and scientific knowing are simply co-extensive, and that there is therefore a binary option between science and nonsense. The majority opinion among the cultured elite in the West is that the scientific revolution of the seventeenth and eighteenth century was a watershed dividing enlightened modernity from a benighted pre-modernity when religious superstition held sway. The scientistic syllogism implicitly accepted by armies of the young runs something like this: the only legitimate form of knowledge is scientific; religious claims are not presented as the result of scientific investigation or analysis; therefore, religion is not a legitimate form of knowledge. The practical result of this bit of reasoning is that it is pointless to mount arguments in regard to religious doctrine.

Versions of scientism have been present in Western thinking for centuries, but our contemporary form has clear roots in the logical positivism of A.J. Ayer and his ideological allies in the Vienna Circle of the 1920s and 1930s. These theorists defended the view that the meaningfulness of a proposition is a function of that proposition's verifiability or at least falsifiability. That is to say, a claim is meaningful if and only if its truth or falsity can be determined through empirical observation. Thus, the assertions that five hundred people attended a lecture I gave last month or that the earth revolves around the sun are meaningful statements, precisely because observation could either confirm or deny them. Religious propositions, however, such as "God exists," "God's will is being realized in this situation," or "the soul shall live forever," are not so much false (though Ayer and his colleagues think they are false) but meaningless, no more than expressions of the feelings and hopes of those who articulate them. One accordingly might smile at them or frown at them disapprovingly, but one would never endeavor to *argue* about them.

Now, problems with this scientistic or positivistic method abound, but the most fundamental difficulty is that the entire program rests squarely upon a contradiction. The principle is that the only meaningful statements are those that can be confirmed through empirical observation and experimentation; and yet, that very principle is not confirmable in such a manner. Where or how does one observe or experimentally verify the assertion that meaningfulness is reducible to that which can be observed through the senses? In point of fact, scientism itself is not scientific but rather philosophical, for it is a rational intuition regarding the epistemological order. Fair enough—but the one thing you are not permitted to accomplish through a philosophical proposal is to exclude philosophical proposals from the category of meaningfulness! Logical positivism, and its contemporary cousin scientism, cut off the branch on which they are sitting; or, to shift the metaphor, they are quite obviously hoisted on their own petard.

A second crucial problem with this proposal is that it stands athwart the practically universal consensus that there are indeed nonscientific paths to knowledge. Who can seriously doubt that philosophy, literature, drama, poetry, painting, and mysticism are not only uplifting and entertaining but also truth-bearing? *Hamlet* provides no real insight into human psychology and motivation? Dante's *Divine Comedy* conveys no truths about politics, art, sin, or religious aspiration? *The Waste Land* tells us nothing intellectually substantive about the human heart? Plato's dialogues shed no real light on ethics, justice, and the good life? One would have to be extremely narrow-minded to think so.

I should like to linger with the example of Plato for a moment. The man who effectively founded the discipline of philosophy in the West understood, as did many other sages and mystics of both the East and West, the beguiling quality of what is given to sense experience. What we can see, touch, taste, hear, and experience directly is so immediately and indisputably there that we can remain completely under its spell. Mind you, Plato did not think that the sensible order is unreal. But he did indeed intuit that there are dimensions of reality that are greater, richer, and more abiding. And he further realized that, in order to gain access to that realm, one must go through a sort of intellectual and spiritual training, or if I might state it more bluntly, a discipline by which one is wrenched away from one's preoccupation with the physical and the sensual. Pierre Hadot pointed out that Plato was proposing not so much a doctrine (though a set of teachings can be distilled from his writings) but rather a *bios* or an entire way of life, something akin to monasticism. The famous dialogues are literary records of the process.

Central to Plato's discipline was conversation, the asking and answering of questions, designed to tease all the participants into a consciousness of the abiding things that lie behind and beyond immediate experience. The literary device that best delineates this progressive illumination is the allegory of the cave found in book seven of the *Republic*. Everyone who has passed through a Philosophy 101 course undoubtedly remembers the main points of the story. A group of prisoners are chained deep inside a cave, compelled by their bonds to face the wall of the cavern on which flicker shadows cast by puppets, which are manipulated by people whom the prisoners cannot see. One of the captives manages to free himself. He turns around and sees the extraordinarily substantive objects, which are the source of the two-dimensional shades that he had taken to be the whole of reality. In time, he wanders past the puppets and makes his way to the mouth of the cave. Venturing outside, he is first overwhelmed by the brightness of the sunlight, but as his eyes adjust, he sees the people, trees, animals, and objects of which the puppets within the cave, he realizes, are but simulacra. Finally, he catches a fleeting glimpse of the sun, in whose light those splendid things appear.

This compelling little tale—which has been mimicked from Dante's *Divine Comedy* to *Fahrenheit 451* and *The Matrix*—is the account of a hero's journey from limited to unrestricted consciousness, from a preoccupation with the immediate to a consideration of the eternal. The flickering shadows and the insubstantial puppets represent the world of sense experience. What subsists in space and time—what can be verified through the senses—is necessarily fleeting, evanescent. Plants, animals, human beings, subatomic particles, and even the stars and planets all come into being and pass out of being. However, a philosophically disciplined conversation discloses that these passing realities are conditioned by a formal dimension of being, represented by the substantive objects and figures outside the cave. Followed all the way to the end, the philosophical quest conduces toward the knowledge of the absolute source from which even the formal feature of being comes—namely, the Good itself—symbolized by the overwhelming beauty of the sun.

Obviously, the spelling out of this process would take us far beyond the purview of this book and into the full complexity of Plato's philosophy. But I might give some flavor of the Platonic approach with one simple example. When a person comes to grasp a mathematical truth, say that 2+3=5, she has, in a very real sense, stepped into another world. As mentioned, everything in sense experience is fleeting, and therefore our knowledge of this realm is extremely limited, unsure, and time-conditioned. It is indeed like watching shadows flicker on a wall. But two and three equal five anytime, anywhere, and in any possible world. To see two things juxtaposed with three things so as to form a conglomerate of five is something any animal could do; but to grasp the principle that two and three are five is to enter a qualitatively higher realm of existence and thought. The commonness of the experience—any first grader can have it—should not blind us to the surpassing significance of it. It is like stepping out of a cave into the light. And the mathematical, for Plato, is but the first step on the way toward properly philosophical perception of the structuring elements of reality.

Plato's best-known pupil, Aristotle, followed the dialogic discipline and came to these deeper perceptions, though he expressed the progress more prosaically than his master. In his mature writings, Aristotle would speak of three different degrees of knowledge: physics, mathematics, and metaphysics. The first studies matter in motion; the second explores numeric and geometrical abstractions; and the third looks into "being as being"—that is to say, the elements that make something not only material or mobile but existent. Aristotle doesn't despise physics for a moment (in fact, it could be credibly argued that he is the father of the discipline), but he insists that the mind pushes past what physics can deliver. As a young man, he had experienced the intoxication of escaping from the cave, and he had no interest in limiting himself to that narrow space.

All of which brings me back to scientism. I reverence the sciences and I benefit daily from the technologies that they've made possible. Moreover, my life has quite literally been saved at least twice by medical interventions that would have been unthinkable before the rise of the modern physical sciences. But even the most advanced, complex, and practically beneficial science is, in Platonic terms, a gazing at shadows on the wall of the cave. It is a useful and beautiful exercise of the mind indeed, but it is a concentration on reality at a relatively low level of intensity. I rarely agree with the well-known atheist Bertrand Russell, but I have always resonated with his comment that mathematics is one of the doors to mysticism and religion. Though he meant that in a reductive and dismissive way, I would affirm its veracity in the Platonic sense: the understanding of a mathematical truth is a first step out of mere sensuality and toward the properly transcendent. The contemporary philosopher Charles Taylor speaks of the "buffered self" as one of the marks of our secular, post-religious culture. By this he means a self sealed off from any contact with the transcendent. Scientism is the official philosophy of the buffered self. Blowing some holes in that barrier and letting in some light is a propaedeutic to having a real argument about religion.

CHAPTER THREE

Be Intolerant of Toleration

ONE OF THE MOST revered ideas in the contemporary West is tolerance, especially in regard to religion. Concomitantly, one of the very worst insults that you can hurl at someone today in our cultural context is that he or she is intolerant of others. Though, as I will argue, there is something deeply right in all of this, the hyper-valorization of tolerance has proven to be a major block to constructive argument about religious matters. For in our postmodern society, toleration of religion typically goes hand in hand with the radical privatization of religion, the relegating of faith to the arena of interiority and its practice to the level of a hobby. Though we might speak with enthusiasm of our passion for boating or golf or poker, no one would be tempted to mount a public argument that everyone ought to be passionate about such activities.

Theologian Stanley Hauerwas has maintained that the contemporary regime of tolerance has its roots in the ideological and political settlements that followed the devastating wars of religion in the aftermath of the Reformation. Because Protestants and Catholics couldn't adjudicate their disputes about doctrine, religious practice, and authority through reason, they resorted to violence—in fact, violence on such a colossal scale that the economic and political stability of Europe was undermined. Therefore, once the dust settled, a sort of deal was struck between state and church. Governments essentially said to religions, we will tolerate you as long as you privatize yourselves and stop making such a public nuisance. Accordingly, many of the political constitutions that emerged after the revolutions of the eighteenth and nineteenth centuries ratified a separation of church and state and established a general liberty of religion.

Furthermore, almost all of the great philosophers of the early modern period—Descartes, Spinoza, Leibniz, Kant, and Jefferson, among many others—advocated some form of rational religion that would effectively relativize the doctrinal differences among the various faith traditions, and hence justify the toleration called for by the political leaders of the time. Someone in whom these two strands came together seamlessly was the great seventeenth-century thinker John Locke, whose *Reasonableness of Christianity* is a classic of rationalistic deism and whose *Letter Concerning Toleration* provided a template for some of the most important constitutional arrangements of modernity. Locke, persuasively enough, argued that religious toleration was good for religion, since no authentic conversion can be compelled through legal constraint. And he held that such broad acceptance is legitimate precisely because the goal of the state (fostering the common public good) and the goal of religion (the saving of souls) are qualitatively different. Here we sense the beginnings of the privatization of religion, the exclusion of faith from the public sphere or the arena of the common good. Religion is granted a sort of privilege by the state, but a heavy price is paid.

What commenced in Locke gained momentum throughout the modern period. One thinks of the move in the nineteenth century, so abhorred by John Henry Newman, to exclude religion from the circle of academic disciplines on the presumption that religion had to do with private and subjective matters. And one certainly thinks of the political theorizing of Jürgen Habermas, John Rawls, and their numerous disciples in the twentieth and twenty-first centuries. Exquisitely attuned to the many ways that our acts of communication become distorted through exclusion and domination, Habermas sought to lay out the conditions for the possibility of "ideal" speech acts. These qualities include radical freedom of discourse, a predilection toward nonviolence and noncoerciveness, a prejudice in favor of open argument, an assumption of the equality of all participants in the conversation, and tolerance of all points of view. Though these never obtain completely, Habermas is convinced that they represent a norm that ought to be approached, albeit asymptotically. But here's the rub. The strict adherence to these prescriptions means that appeals to authority or to special revelations are ruled out. We must give up, Habermas says, "mythological world views . . . which take on legitimating functions for the occupants of positions of authority." This is, of course, a thinly veiled exclusion of religious persons and religious points of view from the table of conversation. Though it can be practiced privately, religion must not intrude upon the open and secular debate of the public arena.

John Rawls, the massively influential American political philosopher, moved along similar lines. He proposed that a perfectly just society would be one established by public-minded people operating behind what he famously termed "a veil of ignorance." This means that the constructors of just social arrangements would, as it were, blind themselves to their own private points of view, prejudices, and understandings of the world, so as not to impose illegitimately on others. They would accept only the most abstract principles of fairness that could be reasonably applied to everyone, no matter their particular preferences and viewpoints. Once again—though it could certainly be tolerated as a private practice—religion, practically by definition, couldn't play a role in the determination of the just social order. As many have indicated, the rhetoric of "freedom of worship" (rather than "freedom of religious practice") used by many politicians on the scene today reflects Rawls' distinctive philosophy of public life.

I don't think it is the least bit accidental that the "new atheist" movement emerged in the immediate wake of the events of September 11th. The attacks of that terrible day confirmed in the minds of many cultural commentators the Enlightenment-era intuition that because religion is irrational, it is necessarily violent. Because they can't solve their differences through argument, religious people have recourse only to aggression. It is furthermore no accident that the most prominent of these critics of religion would, therefore, also advocate for the starkest possible separation between religion and public life. Christopher Hitchens, the best known of the new atheists, cried out once at a public debate, referencing Thomas Jefferson's famous metaphor: "Mr. Jefferson, build up that wall!" All of this theorizing about the need to privatize religion—from Locke to Hitchens—has trickled down into the minds of most young people today, who take it as more or less axiomatic.

The problem, however, is this: religions cannot be privatized precisely because they make truth claims, and the truth, by its very nature, is a public reality. It would be ludicrous to say, "I have a personal conviction that in a right triangle the square of the hypotenuse is equal to the sum of the squares of the other two sides." And it would be equally absurd to say, "But I completely respect the fact that this might not be true for you." Such statements are validly made in regard to matters of personal taste, but they are entirely inappropriate when matters of truth and falsity are under discussion. Religious claims are not mere expressions of personal feeling. They are assertions that something is in fact the case: God exists; God cares providentially for the universe; the soul is immortal; Jesus is the Son of God, who rose from the dead; the sacraments are visible signs that give grace; the direct and intentional killing of innocent human life is intrinsically evil; etc. And let's face it: major religions make assertions that are incompatible with one another. A Christian says that Jesus is divine, and a Muslim denies it. They cannot both be right. Jews deny that God is a Trinity of persons, and Christians affirm it. Someone has to be wrong. Catholics assert that Jesus is really, truly, and substantially present in the Eucharist, and most Protestants say that the Lord's presence in the sacrament is symbolic. Those are mutually exclusive claims.

So what do we do? As I signaled at the outset, I don't think we're doomed to the binary option of bland tolerance or forceful imposition. Rather, argument—public, spirited, deeply respectful, and clear—is called for. Here I will take a page from Locke, Habermas, and Rawls and insist that noncoerciveness is an indispensable prerequisite for productive conversation. And I say this not so much as a modern but as a Christian. If I were to press the case for Jesus Christ, the prince of peace and unambiguous advocate of nonviolence and forgiveness, through threats and intimidation, I would quite simply undermine myself. Have religious people in general, and Christians in particular, been guilty of this sort of tragically contradictory behavior? Absolutely—and I say it to our shame.

But the tragedies and mistakes of the past needn't set the template for our present conversation. At the close of this section, I am going to propose Thomas Aquinas as a splendid model of public, rational argument regarding matters religious, but for the moment, might I bring forward a few examples of more recent vintage? In the middle of the nineteenth century, passionate abolitionists emerged in the United States, arguing vigorously and publicly against the institution of slavery. Though they employed the language of philosophy and social theory to a degree, their case rested for the most part on biblical principles. Though he was never an abolitionist in the strict sense, Abraham Lincoln shared many of the principles of the movement, and when he attempted to articulate the meaning of the Civil

War in his Second Inaugural Address, he used explicitly biblical language of judgment, providence, and moral reckoning. Though Lincoln and the abolitionists met with strenuous opposition for many years—including massive and organized military opposition—in time, their point of view came to be accepted so thoroughly that now the defense of slavery would be seen as tantamount to madness.

Commencing in the early decades of the twentieth century, and culminating in the 1950s and 1960s, a great civil rights movement emerged in the United States. Its most articulate leader, Martin Luther King Jr., argued against segregation and racism in a very public manner. Like his abolitionist forebears, he utilized philosophical and political rhetoric, but the lion's share of his argumentation was biblical in form and inspiration. Speaking in August of 1963 on the steps of the Lincoln Memorial in Washington, DC, King marshaled the language, cadences, and moral principles of the Bible to make his case for racial justice. The "I Have a Dream" speech was not a sermon; it was a political address. But its author did not feel that he had to relegate his religious faith to the private and subjective sphere. He knew that certain truth claims were central to his Christianity, and he did not hesitate to argue for them in the full glare of publicity. Though King met with finally murderous opposition, his argument proved so persuasive that today only the worst extremists would advocate for segregation and racial discrimination.

These instances demonstrate that public religious discourse need not be violent and can prove remarkably persuasive over time. Indeed, to relegate religious claims to the arena of fuzzy subjectivity is essentially to give up on one's interlocutors. Argument is the way to turn even fierce opponents into allies.

CHAPTER FOUR

Avoid Voluntarism

I T HAS BEEN SAID that Gnosticism is the oldest and most enduring heresy in the life of the Christian Church, and a case can definitely be made for this. But I believe that the most powerful and influential heresy today is voluntarism—which is to say, the trumping of intellect by will. To state it a bit more simply, voluntarism is the view that things are true because I want them to be true. I don't know any funnier (or more pathetic) exemplification of voluntarism than a video that went viral about a year ago. An interviewer, who was a white male about six feet tall, made his way around an unnamed American college campus and spoke at random to students. He asked them, "What if I told you that I was a woman?" To a person, every student he spoke to replied, more or less, "If that's what you discern you are, then I'm okay with that." Then he pressed the matter: "What if I told you that I felt I was a Chinese woman?"

Again, without hesitation, each student said, "Well, that's what you are." Finally, he inquired, "What if I told you that I claim the identity of a six-foot-five-inch Chinese woman?" At this point, a few of his interlocutors balked, but in the end, they all agreed that they would be fine with that description if that's what he truly felt he was. In their minds, evidently, gender, race, and even height were not objective states of affairs but a function of subjective desire.

What should be clear even to the most sympathetic observer is that these young people are in the grips of a deeply distorting ideology, one that is not only distancing them from reality, but also making real argument about most matters of importance, including religion, virtually impossible. If reality shifts and drifts according to the wills of individuals, then we can never get a grip on it together; we can never inhabit the same intellectual space long enough to have a conversation.

The roots of this perspective are old and tangled, stretching back at least to the late Middle Ages. In that period, certain philosophers emerged, most notably John Duns Scotus and William of Ockham, who argued for a maximalist understanding of God's power. God's free will determines, they maintained, the nature of reality in all of its dimensions. Hence, things exist because God wills their existence; mathematical truths obtain because God so desires; and ethical principles are valid because God says so. Thus, the Pythagorean theorem holds true because God so decided, but in principle, it might become false if God changes his mind. Similarly, adultery is wrong because God so decreed, but through a shift in God's will, it might become a virtue.

This voluntarism, this extreme emphasis on God's *potentia absoluta* (absolute power), represented a departure from the view of Thomas Aquinas and many others, who refused to drive a wedge between God's being, mind, and will. I cannot, within the confines of this short book, explore this counter-position more thoroughly, but suffice it to say that these perspectives remained at odds until the dawn of the modern period, when voluntarism got the upper hand. One of the avenues by which it came into the heart of Western culture was the writings of the Protestant Reformers, who were largely trained in philosophical schools where voluntarism held sway. If you doubt me, look into the views of both Martin Luther and John Calvin on the predestination of both saints and sinners.

As is often the case in the history of ideas, a strong position tends to awaken an equally strong opposition, and this happened as the modern philosophers went about their work. A God seen as oppressive and arbitrary in his freedom was placed at a far remove from the world by the deists. He was basically identified with the universe by Spinoza; he was collapsed into the sovereign self by Hegel; and he was spiritualized into neutrality by romantics such as Schleiermacher and Emerson. But soon enough, thinkers saw no need for the voluntarist God at all, construing him rightly enough as the enemy of human flourishing and ushering him, with some fanfare, off the stage. Thus Feuerbach declared his atheism with the shout, "The no to God is the yes to man." Marx did so with the slogan, "Religion is the opium of the masses." And Nietzsche's "madman" would cry, "God is dead, and we killed him." Just as the voluntarist God is endowed with *potentia absoluta*, so the voluntarist self wields value and truth-creating power. No one articulated this more clearly than Nietzsche, who extolled the *Ubermensch* (super-man), a hero in whom the will to power is so intense that it shatters any moral and intellectual systems that would constrain it. Jordan Peterson is right to point out that the elimination of God and the concomitant liberation of the human will was not perceived by Nietzsche himself as something altogether exhilarating. On the contrary, he saw that it opened up an abyss.

However, many of Nietzsche's deeply influential successors in the twentieth century were not as reticent. In a presentation he gave in Paris just after the Second World War, Jean-Paul Sartre, the founder of existentialism, endeavored to provide a brief introduction to his controversial philosophy. Later published as a small book called *Existentialism Is a Humanism*, this essay has set the tone, I believe, for much of the thinking of our culture today, even in popular circles. Sartre argued that for most of Western history, at least since the time of Plato, essence was seen as having precedence over existence. This means that certain forms, values, and principles of meaning (essence) come first, and the drama of a well-lived life is the conforming of one's will and behavior (existence) to these objectivities. Sartre turns this scenario upside down, asserting that existence precedes essence. Human freedom comes first, and then, on its own terms, posits meaning, value, and purpose. Therefore, the drama of a life well lived is decidedly not the conformity of freedom to objective truth, but rather the achievement of "authenticity"—that is to say, a subjectivity true to itself.

Though the culture and the state are crucial representatives of the objective normativity that must be de-throned if freedom is to find true expression, the prime bearer of "essence," Sartre taught, is God. Hence, in line with his Nietzschean proclivities, Sartre declared that atheism is (pardon the expression) essential to existentialism. But whereas the death of God produced some misgivings in his German teacher, it struck Sartre as logically required by the new philosophy. He expressed this requirement with syllogistic directness: "If God exists, I cannot be free; but I am free; therefore, God does not exist." If this seems like so much abstract speculation, take a serious look at the decision of the United States Supreme Court in 1992 in the matter of *Planned Parenthood v. Casey*. In deciding for the unrestricted right to abortion, the justices made a sweeping philosophical claim, utterly congruent with Sartrean assumptions: "It belongs to the nature of liberty to determine the meaning of life, of existence, and of the universe." It would be difficult to imagine a more thoroughgoing statement of voluntarism in its Nietzschean form.

When I was a doctoral student in Paris many years ago, the owlish visage of Michel Foucault looked out from practically every bookstore window in the city. He was the most obvious successor to Sartre as a public intellectual, and like his French forebear, he was also a disciple of Nietzsche. But whereas Sartre focused particularly on Nietzsche's atheism and anthropology of self-creation, Foucault put special stress on the German's philosophy of power. In meticulous studies of penal institutions, madness, and sexuality, Foucault endeavored to show that what are taken to be objective moral norms are, in fact, carefully disguised means by which certain groups assert their power. The proof is that these apparently absolute standards vary dramatically from place to place and from period to period. Once more, in line with voluntarist assumptions, the will to self-assertion appears to trump and relativize what are taken to be enduring, transhistorical truths.

I realize these are high philosophical notions, aired originally in sophisticated universities and salons; yet one would have to be deaf and blind not to notice how thoroughly they have permeated the general culture of the early twenty-first century. "Who are you to tell me what to think or how to behave?" "Stop imposing your values on me." "I have the freedom to determine the kind of person I want to be." "What you're telling me is just an attempt to control me." "The so-called permanent things are part of the system by which the powerful maintain their position and suppress the voices of the marginalized." These familiar statements—heard anywhere that young, and not-so-young, people gather—witness to the extraordinary influence of the voluntarism of Nietzsche, Sartre, Foucault, and their countless disciples among university faculties, editorial boards, and the mavens of the popular culture.

You might be wondering, "What does all of this have to do with the posing of religious arguments?" In a word, everything. For when voluntarism holds sway, there is no room for argument, for truth has become utterly individualized and relativized. When the will of each person is absolute, the possibility for constructive conversation on a shared basis evanesces, and all that is left is a clash of freedoms. On Nietzschean terms, bringing forward a proposition as true can only be construed as a power play and hence can (and must) be opposed by a greater assertion of power. Can you see how the adoption of voluntarism has directly transformed our public spaces—especially institutions of higher learning—into ideological battlefields? No one *argues* anymore; they shout one another down and claim victim status.

CHAPTER FIVE

Seek to Understand Your Opponent's Position

AFTER A GOOD DEAL of rather high philosophizing, I'd like to explore a more practical matter in this next brief chapter. As I mentioned at the outset, I have been engaging in discussions and arguments in the internet space for many years, and I've learned, often from painful experience, what makes my interventions either useful or harmful. Far too frequently, feeling the sting of a rebuke or an insulting counter-argument, I will dash off a response that is more vitriolic than clarifying. Or perhaps, eager to show off my intellectual acumen, I will dismantle a poorly-worded observation, indifferent to the fact that a real person stands behind the bland words on the screen. When such moves are made, argument disappears.

Therefore, I recommend as a necessary condition for constructive religious dialogue that all participants put their egos aside and listen to one another, seeking truly to understand the other's position and point of view. This discipline accomplishes a number of important things. First, it allows passionate feelings to subside. I'm in favor of feelings, and I certainly understand that religion stirs them up, but I also know that passionate emotion can obfuscate matters and obscure the light of reason. Simply asking one's interlocutor, in a dispassionate manner, to clarify her position functions as something of a "time-out" and permits a more reasoned exchange to unfold. Secondly, it shows respect for the person who wrote the words, which does both you and him good, for a disrespected person isn't likely to listen and isn't likely to receive your best attention. Thirdly, it allows the question or observation to be further refined so that a response can be more focused and helpful. I have discovered, again through lots of front-line experience, that it might require five or six exchanges before an interlocutor and I really come to the heart of the matter. John Henry Newman observed that ideas do not exist on the printed page but rather in the "play of lively minds." When we take an idea in, we do not dumbly receive it, but instead, we turn it over, look at it from different angles, tease out its implications, etc. And then, in the manner of a game, we toss it back to a fellow player, who does much the same thing. In this sifting process, all of an idea's aspects are allowed to come into the light. Jumping on a question or a challenge with a put-down or a quip or a canned argument simply shuts down this indispensable process.

When I was in the seminary in the 1980s, the psychology of Carl Rogers was all the rage in pastoral formation. At least in the somewhat simplified version I was taught, Rogers encouraged any counselor or therapist to respond to a client with "unconditional positive regard" and to mirror back what he heard the client saying in conversation. For example: "It sounds like this is a very painful situation for you," or "What I hear you saying is that your husband is really not paying attention to you." This two-pronged approach, Rogers held, would allow the analysand's hidden feelings and fears to surface.

Far be it from me to recommend this approach uncritically, but I do believe elements of it can be helpful in the context of religious argument and debate. As a response to even a sharply-worded challenge, one might say, for instance, "What I think I hear you saying is that profound human suffering is just not compatible with the claim that God is infinite love," or "I sense the concern behind your question is that belief in God will lead to an attenuating of human responsibility," or "Am I right in supposing that you're wondering whether one can reconcile the classical arguments for God with the findings of contemporary science?" There is an excellent chance that your opponent is saying something right, that she is putting forward, however awkwardly or angrily, a perspective that many extremely smart people have advocated over the centuries. In regard to philosophical and religious matters, there inevitably obtains a certain complexity and obscurity, and there are rarely knock-down arguments. Acknowledging all such subjects with humility and a touch of humor can go a long way toward establishing the conditions for the possibility of a fruitful exchange.

The great Protestant theologian Paul Tillich famously characterized religion as one's "ultimate concern." A person is concerned about many things—her family's well-being, her bank accounts, how her children are doing in school, who will be the next president, etc.—but amidst all of these proximate preoccupations, there is necessarily something that concerns her unconditionally, without restriction, something that is of ultimate value to her. This is her religion. Therefore, when broaching a religious topic, we must realize that we are treading on very holy ground indeed, on that which is of supreme importance to our interlocutor. If we say something that runs counter to her assumptions in this area, we oughtn't to be surprised that she responds vehemently, passionately, even a tad irrationally. Far, far too often, those who enter the virtual space and endeavor to have a religious conversation clomp around aggressively, indifferent to the passionate feelings that necessarily accompany the religious convictions of their conversation partners. We should tread lightly when treating of religion; we should take off our shoes on holy ground.

CHAPTER SIX
Follow the Example of Thomas Aquinas

AS I BRING this first section of the book to a close, I would like to propose a concrete model for rational, sane, public, and fruitful religious argument. Though it might surprise the numberless people who take the modern framework to be most helpful in this regard, I hearken back to the Middle Ages and to a figure probably little known to most citizens of the digital world today. I am speaking of Thomas Aquinas. Thomas was, by common consensus, the greatest of the doctors (teachers) who flourished in the newly-born university system of thirteenth-century Europe. There had been, to be sure, a rich intellectual life within the monastic schools of the Christian world prior to this time, but commencing in the early 1200s, in places like Naples, Padua, Oxford, Bologna, and Paris, proper universities arose, institutions in which the full array of academic disciplines were cultivated. Unlike the more staid monastic schools that they supplanted, the medieval universities were urban and cosmopolitan, and the style of thought on offer there was edgier, more rational, and more skeptical. Think of the difference between Anselm of Canterbury and Abelard of Paris to get a sense of the change.

Aquinas became a *magister* (master or professor) of theology at the University of Paris around the year 1250, when he was no more than twenty-five, and he rapidly established himself as the most skillful intellectual combatant of that time and place. I use the term "combatant" on purpose, for the principal means of teaching in the medieval university was not the classroom lecture with which we are familiar, but rather the *quaestio disputata* (the disputed question), which was a public debate, a lively and sometimes raucous intellectual exchange between masters and disciples. Typically, a *magister* would propose a topic for consideration—say, the divinity of Jesus, or the virtues, or the power of God—and then a crowd made up of students, other professors, and interested bystanders would gather. The master would first entertain objections from the floor ("Jesus cannot be divine, for the Scriptures consistently emphasize his humanity," or "God cannot be all-powerful, for there are certain things that he cannot do") and then respond as best he could on the spur of the moment. The next day, the same community would come together, and this time the master, having considered all the objections and clarified his own thinking, would deliver his final resolution of the issue.

I realize that the written texts of Thomas can seem dry in the extreme, but we have to recall that they are literary distillations of *quaestiones disputatae*, those energetic, free-wheeling conversations. If we consult Aquinas' masterpiece, the *Summa theologiae*, we find accounts of hundreds upon hundreds of these centuries-old debates. Perhaps the first thing that a reader of Aquinas notices is precisely the range and freedom of his mind. Not only does he ask countless questions, but it appears that nothing is off the table, the best evidence of which is article three of question two of the first part of the *Summa*: "*Utrum Deus sit?*" ("Whether God exists?"). If a Dominican friar is permitted to pose that question, everything is fair game; nothing is too dangerous to talk about. After stating the issue, Thomas then entertains a series of objections to the position that he will eventually take. In many cases, these reflect the real questions and counter-claims he would have heard from the floor during *quaestiones disputatae*, but for our purposes, the point to emphasize is that Thomas invariably presents these objections in their most convincing form, often stating them more pithily and persuasively than their advocates would have done.

In proof of this generosity, we note that during the Enlightenment, rationalist *philosophes* would sometimes take Thomas' objections and use them to bolster their own anti-religious positions! If you want just one example of this resolute refusal to engage in straw-man argumentation, consider Thomas' devastatingly convincing formulation of the argument from evil for the nonexistence of God: "If one of two contraries be infinite, the other would be altogether destroyed; but God is called the infinite good. Therefore, if God exists, there would be no evil. But there is evil. Therefore, God does not exist." Now, Thomas would indeed provide a telling response to that objection, but it remains a wickedly good argument. Might I suggest that our religious discussions today would be far more fruitful if all parties would be willing to formulate their opponents' positions as respectfully and convincingly as possible?

Having articulated the objections, Thomas then offers his own magisterial resolution of the matter in the so-called *Respondeo* (I respond). I have been insisting that the medieval intellectual conversation was open-ended, free-wheeling, willing to take on any question, and marked by vigorous disagreement; but it was decidedly not characterized by our postmodern shillyshallying, the endless postponement of anything like a definitive *answer* to a question. Whereas many today fear that intellectual resolution is tantamount to exclusion or giving offense, Thomas knew what Chesterton knew: that an open mind is like an open mouth, designed finally to bite down on something solid and nourishing. An intellectual decision (from the Latin *de-caedere*, to cut off) is always a somewhat bloody affair, for it means that every rival opinion is disallowed. But without such resolution, any conversation wanders into flippancy. After spelling out his response, Aquinas finally returns to the original objections and, in light of his resolution, answers them. It is notable that Thomas' typical technique is to find something right in the objector's position and to use that to correct what is errant in it. Once again, he displays an extraordinary generosity of mind, accentuating the positive and cajoling rather than steamrolling his opponent.

Throughout this entire process—in the articulation of objections, in the formulation of the *Respondeo*, and in the answer to objections—Thomas draws on a stunning range of sources: the Bible and the Church Fathers to be sure, but also classical philosophers such as Aristotle, Plato, and Cicero, the Jewish scholar Moses Maimonides, and Islamic thinkers such as Averroes, Avicenna, and Avicebron. And he consistently invokes these figures with supreme respect, characterizing Aristotle as simply "the Philosopher" and referring to Maimonides as "Rabbi Moyses." It is certainly fair to say that Thomas Aquinas disagrees with all of these interlocutors in substantial ways; and yet he is more than willing to listen to them, engage them, and take their arguments seriously.

What the Thomistic method produces, if I can borrow the language of our time, is a "safe space" for religious conversation, but a safe space for adults and not for timorous children. It is indeed marked by broad-mindedness, deep respect, the raising of any and all questions, and the inclusion of diverse voices;

but it is a place where truth is sought and claimed. Might I modestly suggest that it would not be a bad model for our present discussion of the most serious things?

Section Two

RELIGION AND THE
OPENING UP OF THE MIND

A TERM THAT DID NOT EXIST when I was a child but which is common parlance today is "search engine." There are dozens, if not hundreds, of these complex tools designed to scour the World Wide Web for information. Google, Yahoo, Bing, and many others give us something that our ancestors could only imagine in their wildest fantasies: practically instant access to most of the information available to the human race. The press of a button can give me an article from the *Summa theologiae* of Aquinas, the entire *Divine Comedy* of Dante, a detailed summary of the theory of relativity, the Spanish word for "dance," the final score of game three of the 1937 World Series, and all of the characters on "F Troop." Whatever our minds (if not our hearts) desire is readily available for our consumption.

This moment in our civilizational development has an intriguing connection to religion. It is a curious feature of our intellects that they restlessly, even relentlessly, seek. By a very deeply-rooted instinct, we want to know, and accordingly, we stubbornly ask questions and endeavor to find answers. But when we come upon the answers we searched out, we aren't satisfied; rather, dozens more questions emerge, frequently ones we never thought we had. We might rest for a moment in our intellectual searching, but this is akin to the brief repose of a climber on the side of the mountain: fleeting, impermanent, just a chance to catch our breath. In accord with this instinct, I have often spent substantial periods of time on the computer, following a line of questioning, moving from site to site, exploring themes I originally had no intention of exploring, only to find them more compelling than what I had first endeavored to learn. And this questing, quite obviously, goes infinitely beyond what is strictly necessary for biological survival. Whereas an animal would use his intelligence or follow his instinct in order to find a handful of basic goods, a human being wants to know any number of completely impractical and useless things: philosophical truths, the aesthetic dimension of reality, purely abstract mathematics, etc. To see this as simply an epiphenomenon of the evolutionary drive to survival strikes me as hopelessly reductionistic.

In his epistemological theorizing, Thomas Aquinas speaks of the *intellectus agens* (the agent intellect). Since the Latin term *agens* is a present participle, a more accurate rendering might be "the searching mind" or "the acting mind." The senses, he says, take in basic data; the imagination holds them for contemplation; and then the *intellectus agens* commences to analyze them, relentlessly asking the question, "*Quid sit?*" ("What might that be?"). When it discovers an answer, it immediately recognizes that answer as incomplete and provisional, and so it asks again, "*Quid sit?*" This stubborn questioning is apparent in any child, until we shame her out of it or discourage her sufficiently—but on and on the mind goes, striving to grasp the fullness of truth. For instance, my senses and imagination present my computer keyboard to my agent intellect for consideration. My restless mind wonders what this might be and formulates the answer: a device for transferring data to my computer screen. But what is a device for transferring data to a computer screen? It is a type of machine. And what is a machine? It is a physical object manufactured for a concrete purpose. And what is that? It is a physical thing. And what is a physical thing? Is it a type of reality? And what does it mean to say that a thing is real? By a series of simple questions, the mind has moved upward and outward from a very particular object to the horizon of all that can be known, to the infinite sea of being itself. Bernard Lonergan summed this up by saying that the mind ultimately wants to know "everything about everything"; or, to put the same idea in more explicitly theological language, it seeks the beatific vision, the vision of God—not one more true thing, but Truth itself, truth in its unconditioned form. Though the mind is empty to begin with, it is the emptiness of a stomach, not the emptiness of a box. That is to say, though the mind has no positive content in it from the outset, it is not dumbly passive, simply waiting to be filled up; rather, it knows what it wants and actively seeks it.

I hope you see now why I hold that there is an intriguing link between search engines and religion. They are both, in a way, functions of the unrestricted desire to know, both tightly correlated to the restlessness of the *intellectus agens*. I would like to state my basic argument in this section bluntly enough at the outset: my most serious objection to secularism and atheism is that they involve the shutting down of the mind. Though skeptics and atheists both old and new tend to wrap themselves in the mantle of reason, I fear that they are, in point of fact, enemies of reason, precisely in the measure that they drop or rule out of court the most interesting questions. They lock the spirit within the confines of the "buffered self" I referenced earlier, permitting only certain types of questions—namely, those that emerge within a materialistic framework. Though it is regularly excoriated as superstitious and irrational, religion at its best always represents the opening up of the mind, the full engagement of the *intellectus agens*, and the liberation of the spirit. Wittgenstein said that much of philosophy consists in "showing the fly the way out of the fly-bottle"—which is to say, liberating the mind from the narrow and stuffy space in which it has trapped itself for various reasons. Real religion—and not its credulous and naïve simulacrum so often critiqued by rationalists—lets the fly out of the bottle and permits the mind to soar.

CHAPTER SEVEN

An Argument for God's Existence

I SHOULD LIKE TO demonstrate this dynamism first by examining a classical argument for the existence of God. By looking at this demonstration in some detail, I will endeavor to show that the restless mind finds its ultimate purpose not in the contemplation of contingent events and causes but in the quest for ultimate reality. Arguing for God—and not just arguing about things and events in the world—is a characteristic of the *intellectus agens* at its most adventurous.

Human beings have been arguing about the existence of God from time immemorial. Many of our greatest thinkers—Aristotle, Augustine, Anselm, Thomas Aquinas, Bonaventure, Descartes, Leibniz, and Whitehead, to name just a few—have proposed rational demonstrations for God's existence. And practically an equal number of prominent philosophers and scientists—Hume, Feuerbach, Freud, Sartre, Russell, Dawkins, etc.—have claimed confidently to have debunked those demonstrations. Even many devout believers have expressed the concern that making arguments for God is tantamount to idolatry, placing God, as it were, under the control of our schemas of rationality.

In the wake of the "new atheist" critiques at the beginning of the twenty-first century, there has been a renewal of interest in these arguments on the part of both their advocates and their detractors. Though I share the worries of many of my fellow believers that this approach carries the danger of intellectual idolatry, I believe that, on balance, thinking through the demonstrations critically and carefully has been a good thing for the Church—not only for apologetic reasons, but also because such an effort serves to tease the spirit out of a materialistic complacency, to challenge the buffered self.

Many years ago, I read the famous exchange—originally broadcast on radio—between Bertrand Russell, the most prominent atheist of the twentieth century, and F.C. Copleston, the great Jesuit historian of philosophy. Copleston succinctly and convincingly laid out the version of the argument from contingency proposed by Leibniz in the seventeenth century. Then, in the course of many pages, Russell stubbornly refused to engage the argument in any way. Claiming that he thought Copleston's language was unintelligible, he neither agreed nor disagreed. He simply wouldn't play, insisting that looking for a reason for the existence of the universe is silly since, in his words, "the world is just there." My deep frustration with Russell's intransigence came back to my mind often as I read and listened in more recent years to the new atheists. Again and again, when confronted with versions of the cosmological argument, Christopher Hitchens, Richard Dawkins, Sam Harris, and their colleagues would say that "matter is eternal" or "the world just popped into existence out of nothing." If these "answers" strike you as pathetically unsatisfying, you're right. If only to break us out of a materialistic dogma and honor the demands of the questing mind, I believe that arguing for God is a desideratum.

Thomas Aquinas, who was deeply convinced of the danger of intellectual idolatry, never referred to his arguments for God as "proofs," but only as *viae* (paths or ways). He certainly understood any God who could be "proven" in the manner of a geometrical demonstration would hardly be worthy of our worship and would scarcely qualify as the God whom the Bible describes as essentially "hidden." Nevertheless, Thomas thought that the mind could at least be led in the direction of God through the right sort of philosophical instruction—again, in the manner of a *manuductio*, a guiding by the hand.

What I would like to do now is present an argument for God's existence that is not identical to any of Thomas' five from the *Summa theologiae* but which borrows elements from some of them and is, I hope, very much in the spirit of Aquinas. It begins, as do Thomas' first three, with the fact of contingency—which is to say, dependency in the ontological order. Things and states of affairs exist, but they don't have to exist. To put this in more precise language: they exist, but they do so nonnecessarily. Consider for sake of argument the state of affairs that is obtaining as I type these words. It is, to be sure, but it does not have to be. I might never have been born; my computer might have stopped working this morning; I could have decided to do something else; the desk the computer is resting upon might have been damaged; the room I'm in might have been heated to 200 degrees—and I could go on proposing counter-factual conditionals indefinitely. The point is that things could have been otherwise. What this implies, in turn, is that this state of affairs—my sitting at a desk typing—does not contain within itself the sufficient reason for its own existence. It has to be explained through reference to causes extrinsic to itself. (This intuition, by the way, is precisely what undergirds all of the physical sciences. In fact, it is rather intriguing, even mysterious, that every scientist—physicist, chemist, psychologist, biologist—automatically searches out causes for the phenomena she investigates.)

Therefore, my typing these words is a function of extrinsic causes that are, here and now, actualizing a potential, making real what would have been a mere possibility without them. They include (and we've already hinted at this) the temperature of the room in which the computer and I are situated; my state of at least relatively good health; the stability of the desk on which the computer rests; the proper functioning of my neural and muscular systems; the ideas and words that are swimming in my mind and continuously informing my writing; my motivation to finish this book; etc. Having made the determination that a contingent state of affairs is grounded in a set of actualizing causes, our restless intellects naturally enough pose the question: Are those causes themselves caused, or are they self-explanatory? Well, it is rather perfectly obvious that all of the causes that we mentioned are, in fact, contingent. The temperature in the room is a function of the external environment and the heating system within my building; my good health is caused by a range of factors within my organism; the stability of the desk depends upon the stability of the floor on which it rests; the ideas in my mind are conditioned by the synapses in my brain; the motivation to write this book nests, as we saw earlier, in a whole range of wider motivations. Have we settled the question? Hardly. For the simplest reflection reveals that all of these conditions are themselves conditioned: the temperature of the external environment by factors within the atmosphere; the health of my organism by smooth functioning at the cellular level; the stability of the floor by the stability of the earth's surface; etc. And these are conditioned by still more—and on and on. Indeed, the various physical sciences have helped enormously to identify these myriad levels of causes which, even as they actualize others, are themselves being actualized.

Now, what cannot be the case? It cannot be true that these chains of contingent, conditioned causes stretch on indefinitely. For if we suppress the first element in such a chain, we suppress all subsequent causes and hence the state of affairs currently under consideration. To return to our example, if we just go on to infinity, citing instance after instance of actualized actualizers, we never succeed in adequately explaining my act of typing these words. We must conclude, therefore, to some reality that actualizes without being actualized, some first cause of contingent states of affairs. I might lay out this demonstration in short compass as follows: the restless mind is compelled by the principle of sufficient reason, meaning contingent things and events must be adequately accounted for; an infinite regress of caused causes is repugnant to that principle; hence, there must finally be an adequate explanation for the existence of non-self-explanatory states of affairs. This uncaused cause, this noncontingent source of contingent existence, is what we call "God."

In order to clarify the argument, it might be useful to consider some of the standard objections that have been raised to it. There is a persistent misunderstanding of this type of argument, for a first instance, based upon a confusion regarding infinite causal series. Bertrand Russell made the remarkably naïve observation that the original formulators of this argument denied infinite causal regress because they were incapable of imagining an infinite series. Nothing could be further from the truth. Both ancient and medieval thinkers offered nuanced reflections on the infinite. Others suggest that this kind of demonstration depends upon the assumption that time is finite, for if it were otherwise, then an infinite regress of caused causes back into history would be possible. But this is actually neither here nor there, for the kind of causal series under consideration—and all of my examples were meant to confirm this point—is not one that stretches back in time. I am not arguing that I was caused by my father and he by his father and he by his father, until we come finally to a primordial cause at the beginning of time. That sort of series Thomas Aquinas referred to as subordinated *per accidens*, meaning that the causal relationship between the elements is incidental to an actualizing of a potential here and now. For instance, my activity is not here and now dependent on my father or grandfather or great-grandfather, all of whom are absent and, causally speaking, irrelevant.

What Thomas denies—and I am following him—is a series in which each element is here and now dependent upon the influence of a preceding cause. For in this sort of series, ordered *per se* in Thomas' terminology, an infinite regress simply cannot account for a contingent state of affairs that lies before us. Recently, someone sent me a video that purported to present Thomas Aquinas' cosmological argument for God's existence. As the presenter began to speak, I noticed a line of dominoes arrayed before him, and I immediately knew we were heading in the wrong direction. Thomas was not interested so much in a God who may or may not have exerted actualizing influence in the distant past; he was interested—and so am I—in the God in whom, here and now, "we live and move and have our being."

A second perennial objection runs along the following lines. Even if we grant the coherency of the logic of the demonstration, there is no reason to conclude that the uncaused cause, the noncontingent ground of contingency, might not be matter as such, primal energy, or the universe construed as a totality. The critic might observe that although particular things and states of affairs come into being and pass away, matter—the matrix from which they arise and to which they return—remains eternal, unchanging, and unconditioned. But this cannot be right. What the argument concludes to is the existence of some reality whose very nature is to exist and hence whose being is marked by no hint of potentiality. But matter as such or "energy" is supremely potential, for it never exists in some pure undifferentiated state but only as determined by this or that modality. Whenever we speak of matter or energy, we have to specify its velocity, its intensity, its color, its heat, its configuration, its location, etc. This necessarily implies that it has been affected by a cause or collection of causes; consequently, it cannot possibly be the reality to which the argument has pointed. To say that the process of matter affecting matter just goes on endlessly is no good, for it simply reintroduces the infinite regress problem.

Some theorists, influenced by the anomalies inherent in a quantum view of reality, opine that subatomic particles pop into existence "from nothing" all the time, and hence, there is no need to stipulate causes of contingency at all. But this objection is grounded in simple equivocation around the word "nothing." When the quantum physicists say "nothing," they are not referring to the sheer nonbeing targeted by the philosophical use of the term, but rather to a fecund field of energy marked by a variety of properties and potentialities. The "nothing" of the quantum theorists is, in philosophical terms, a contingent state of affairs and hence requires an explanation. There was an amusing but telling moment in the televised debate between the atheist Richard Dawkins and a Catholic bishop from Australia. As Dawkins was carrying on at some length regarding the nothing from which all things presumably came, the audience commenced to laugh. "Why are you laughing?" asked Dawkins in what seemed like genuine amazement. To which the Catholic bishop responded, "Well, I think it's a bit funny to be trying to define nothing!"

A third major objection to this kind of argument is that it leads only to an abstract metaphysical principle and not the personal, passionate Creator described in the Bible. To be sure, not even its most ardent advocates would claim that the argument from contingency delivers an adequate, much less complete, picture of God. Nevertheless, by a few logical moves, one can readily show that there is a deep compatibility between the noncontingent ground of contingency and the God of the Scriptures. As the unconditioned source of contingent existence, this ultimate reality is quite properly described as the Creator of all things. Moreover, as fully actualized, it cannot be marked by matter, which is radically potential by its very nature. Since time is a measure of change, and since this reality cannot change, it is correctly described as eternal or outside of time. As unconditioned in its being, furthermore, it must be free of any existential imperfection. And since lack of mind, will, freedom, and personhood would necessarily imply imperfection, it must be in possession of all of those features. Thus, the argument has delivered to us someone who is perfect, intelligent, active, immaterial, eternal, and the Creator of all finite things. Perhaps this is not the biblical God in every detail, but it's certainly more than a reasonable facsimile.

I would like to make a final observation regarding the relationship between this kind of demonstration and the work of the sciences. Occasionally one will hear that the argument from contingency is just a desperate appeal to a "god of the gaps." What the critics mean is that the first cause or the unmoved mover is a misleading designation of some gap in our current scientific account of the causes responsible for a given phenomenon. As we steadily understand more and more of the universe and its dynamics, the proponents of God will simply take one step beyond what we know, point into the darkness, and say, "God is responsible." As science advances, "God" beats a pathetic retreat, always one step ahead of the light.

But this is so much nonsense. First, the reality disclosed by the argument from contingency cannot be one existent among many, for it is the unconditioned act of being itself. Hence, it could not, even in principle, function as an element in a conventional causal chain. It could not possibly fit into the "gap" in any system of explanation. When the emperor Napoleon asked the cosmologist La Place precisely how God functioned in the researcher's model of the universe, he received the famous answer: "I have no need of that hypothesis." But all that that exchange revealed is that neither Napoleon nor La Place apparently understood what classical Catholic philosophy means by the word "God." Any reality that could be arranged within the nexus of conditioned causes is not the unconditioned source of the being of the universe itself. Any cause—however impressive—among other causes is not the reason why there is something rather than nothing. If one were to ask how to make a cherry pie, one would expect an answer along these lines: you would need cherries, starch, dough, the heat of the oven, etc. What one ought never to expect is an answer such as this: you need cherries, starch, God, dough, the heat of the oven, etc., as though God were one fussy cause alongside the others. God is the answer to an altogether different kind of question—namely, why are there cherries, starch, dough, and ovens at all?

The second problem with the "god of the gaps" objection is that it rests upon a category error. In the measure that one construes God as filling a gap in a scientific schema of explanation, one fails to grasp that the demonstration is metaphysical rather than physical. The one who develops it is asking and answering a qualitatively different kind of question than those posed by a scientist. Recall what we argued in the first part of the book regarding Plato's cave. The metaphysician has left the cave—which is to say, the evanescent realm of what can be determined through observation and experimentation—and is inquiring after the structures of being as being. The "god of the gaps" accusation is one made by those dwelling inside the cave; those who have already escaped from the cave are seeing a different dimension of reality.

And this brings us to the principal theme of this second section of the book: the opening up of the mind. The affirmation of the existence of the noncontingent ground of contingency is utterly compatible with the unfettered exercise of scientific investigation, for whatever the sciences uncover—even stretching back to the beginning of the cosmos and outward to the edges of the measurable universe—belongs to the realm of contingent existence. Physicists, chemists, biologists, and astronomers can describe finite, empirically verifiable causes and states of affairs as thoroughly as they want, but they will never reach the dimension of being that we have identified as the unconditioned. This is not because the unconditioned lies provisionally outside their grasp, but because it is qualitatively beyond what scientific methods are suited to explore. Though ideological materialists want to limit it to the empirical and the measurable, human intelligence stubbornly poses those questions that surpass even the purview of the sciences. Accordingly, philosophy and religion do not represent a reversion to superstition, but rather an opening up of the restlessly inquiring mind.

CHAPTER EIGHT
Elijah and the Priests of Ba'al

HAVING SHOWN the dynamism of the questing mind, I should like now to broaden the frame of reference a bit and look at the other great faculty of the human spirit—namely, the will. Just as the mind looks restlessly until it finds the truth itself, so the will does not rest until it rests in the good itself. I will demonstrate this opening up of the will not so much through formal argument, but through a biblical story that has proven to be of perennial spiritual value.

In the middle of the first book of Kings, we find a cycle of narratives dealing with the adventures of the prophet Elijah. We know from the accounts of the Transfiguration in the Gospels that Elijah was seen by ancient Israel as the paradigmatic prophet. He flourished in the ninth century BC during the reign of King Ahab and Queen Jezebel, and his name, *Elijahu* in Hebrew, means "Yahweh is my God."

Ahab is described by the author of the first book of Kings as worse than all of the other kings of Israel, which, given the moral turpitude and political incompetence of the majority of those worthies, is saying quite a lot. And Jezebel was a foreigner, a non-Israelite who had brought the worship of alien gods into the nation. Though this issue of idol worship probably strikes us today as rather quaint, it was of crucial importance to the scriptural authors, for on the biblical reading, misdirected praise is always the central moral and spiritual problem, the dysfunction from which all other difficulty and distortion flows. To understand this principle adequately, we have to go back to the very beginning of the Bible, to the opening chapters of the book of Genesis. In describing the orderly procession of all things from the Creator, the poet is deftly making two pivotal points simultaneously. First, he is dethroning all of those realities—sun, moon, planets, stars, mountains, animals, and the earth itself—which were, in various cultures and at various times, worshipped as deities. They are not divine, he is insisting, but creaturely. On the other hand, he is indicating their proper function in the order of creation, precisely by presenting them in a sort of liturgical procession. The whole point of sun, moon, animals, and insects is to give praise to their Creator, to order their existence according to God's purpose. It is of supreme significance that, again in accord with liturgical sensibilities, human beings come last in the procession, for their raison d'être will be the leading of the chorus of creation. When human beings fulfill their priestly role, they will bring their own souls into right order and make possible the right ordering of the material world as well.

The etymology of the word "adoration" is worth pondering in this context. *Adoratio* in Latin is derived from two words, *ad* and *ora*, meaning "to the mouth." The sense is that the stance of adoration is a lining up of our powers to God, literally being mouth-to-mouth with him. When we are so aligned with God—taking in "every word that comes from the mouth of God"—all the elements that make us up fall into harmony, and the world around us finds its proper harmony as well. And by implication, false worship—aligning oneself to something or someone other than God—results in a disintegration of the self and a falling apart of the wider world. The theologian Paul Tillich, whom I referenced in the first section, once commented that all you need to know about a person can be discovered through asking and answering a simple question: What do you worship? Everyone, religious or otherwise, holds something of highest value, places something at the center of his or her life. From that grounding move, everything else follows.

With this sketch in mind, we can look at the story of Elijah and the priests of Ba'al with fresh eyes. Because of the idolatry introduced by Jezebel, we are told that the Lord has sent a drought upon the land. It is supremely important not to read the punishments of God described in the Bible as arbitrary or capricious; rather, we should see them as expressions of fundamental spiritual laws, a sort of physics of the soul. Taking their cue from the beginning of Genesis, the biblical authors often use garden imagery to communicate spiritual flourishing and the desert to indicate the lifelessness that follows upon rejection of God. Hence, the drought at the time of Elijah is a close cousin to the desert into which Adam and Eve were expelled. When we turn from the source of life, engaging in forms of false praise, life dries up in and around us. In the midst of the drought, Elijah is sent to confront King Ahab. It is wonderful that the biblical author tells us practically nothing of Elijah's background or formation. All we learn is the trivial detail that he hails from the little town of Tishbe, about which even specialist scholars know practically nothing. He has come for one purpose, which is summed up by his name. When he enters the King's presence, Ahab remonstrates with him, "Is it you, you troubler of Israel?" But Elijah is having none of it: "I have not troubled Israel; but you have, and your father's house, because you have forsaken the commandments of the Lord and followed the Ba'als."

After this initial exchange, Elijah directly challenges the king: "Now therefore have all Israel assemble for me at Mount Carmel, with the four hundred fifty prophets of Ba'al." On that sacred ground, Elijah proposes to challenge them directly. They are to erect altars to their gods, and Elijah will prepare an altar for the Lord; both will call upon their respective deities; and "the god who answers by fire is indeed God." A first point to note is that the prophets of Ba'al outnumber the prophet of Yahweh four hundred and fifty to one. So it goes across the ages: the representatives of false forms of worship are always thick on the ground, while those who advocate for true praise are typically a tiny minority. St. Augustine expressed the same idea when he opined that the City of God—the community governed by the love of God—is like Noah's ark, tossing on the waves of the mighty ocean of the City of Man, that polity governed by love of self.

In response to Elijah's challenge, the priests of Ba'al cried out all the day long to their god: "O Ba'al, answer us!" But no sound came and no fire fell. They then commenced to dance on and around the altars, but still there was no response. Elijah made bold to mock them: "Cry aloud! Surely he is a god; either he is meditating, or he has wandered away, or he is on a journey, or perhaps he is asleep and must be awakened." Stung, the priests of Ba'al proceed to cut themselves with knives and lances "until the blood gushed out over them. . . . But there was no voice, no answer, and no response." Finally, Elijah—having prepared the altar by covering and surrounding it with water—prays to God: "Answer me, O Lord, answer me, so that this people may know that you, O Lord, are God, and that you have turned their hearts back." With that, fire came down from heaven, lapping up the water and consuming the sacrifice. And all the people fell to the ground in worship.

I realize that a first-time reader of this story might well be tempted to think that it is just another instance of culturally-conditioned, chest-thumping chauvinism ("My God is bigger than your God"). However, what unfolds here is, in fact, a powerful meditation on the central challenge for any human being: How ought I to direct my most fundamental spiritual energies and aspirations? In the elucidation of this question, I don't know a better guide than Thomas Aquinas. The second major section of Aquinas' *Summa theologiae*, which deals in general with the nature of the good life, commences with a consideration of happiness (*beatitudo* in Thomas' Latin). G.K. Chesterton suggested that good morality is like good art; it starts with drawing a line. It's a well-turned phrase, but Thomas wouldn't agree with its import, for he addresses law (the drawing of a line, morally speaking) for the first time only in question ninety of the second part of the *Summa*. His discussion begins not with law but with happiness, that good which everyone, consciously or unconsciously, is ultimately seeking all the time.

Though philosophers and scientists from the dawn of the modern period have been uneasy with the classical idea of final causality in nature (that material things act for an end and are pulled as much as pushed), only the most orthodox determinists would deny that something like final causes exist as far as human motivation is concerned. Our wills are beguiled by goods outside of themselves, which they seek to obtain. For instance, I am entering these words into my computer right now so that I might produce the book that you are reading. But a moment's reflection discloses that that very particular end nests in a further, more englobing purpose: I am endeavoring to write this book so that I can further my work of evangelizing the culture. And that goal rests, Russian-doll-like, in still a higher end: I'm doing the work of evangelizing the culture because I want to bring all people to Christ, and bringing people to Christ fulfills my sense of mission, which makes me happy. The example I've chosen might lead you to believe I've loaded the dice in the direction of religion; but a similar analysis can be done regarding any and all acts of the will, and a fairly mystical finality will inevitably present itself. A person gets out of bed in the morning because she has to get to work; she goes to work in order to earn a salary; she earns a salary in order to have money to support her family; she wants to support her family because she wants them to have material things, a good education, and the opportunity to live without fear; she wants those things because she desires happiness for her loved ones; she wants that because pleasing her family makes *her* happy. Or, even more directly, a man goes to a ballgame to watch his favorite team; he does this because he loves baseball; he loves baseball because baseball makes him happy; and what he wants, finally, is to be happy all the time. Ultimately, Thomas Aquinas argues, all human agents—saints and sinners, the compassionate and the wicked—are motivated by a desire for the joy and peace of *beatitudo*. But surely, one might protest, the professional hitman or the determined mass murderer or the unrepentant child molester is not seeking happiness. But they are indeed, in however distorted a manner. As Thomas puts it with characteristic terseness, even the worst sinner is choosing what appears to him to be good—that is to say, productive of happiness.

And this leads to the obvious question: What precisely *is* authentic beatitude? What is it that truly makes us happy? If we find that, we will have found the holy grail; we will have uncovered the great secret; we will know whom or what to worship. In the opening articles of the second part of the *Summa*,

Thomas examines a number of proposals that have been made in the course of the centuries. Some have suggested that wealth is the ultimate good, that value around which all other values revolve, and I daresay that one might find a number of advocates for this position in our materialistic culture today. Indeed, for many in the contemporary West, wealth seems to be at least an essential component of the good life. But Thomas insists that wealth cannot fulfill this function. There are, he argues, two types of wealth: natural and artificial. The first is that which "serves as a remedy for our natural wants: such as food, drink, clothing, cars, dwellings, and such like." But these things cannot be the ultimate end, for they are subordinated to what Thomas refers to as the "support of human nature"—that is, they sustain a person in health and psychological contentment so that he might turn to higher goods, such as study, friendship, contemplation, etc. The second type of wealth, the artificial variety, is meant simply to acquire natural wealth, and thus is even further removed from the status of ultimate good.

Others have suggested that human beatitude consists in honors. To grasp the weight and import of this suggestion, we should call to mind the number of great societies, both ancient and modern, that are predicated upon honor and shame. In such a community, nothing would be more painful than public humiliation. One could endure the loss of home, wealth, pleasure, and friends, but the loss of face would be unbearable. And this seems to indicate that, at least in such a culture, honor, fame, and reputation would constitute the highest value. But Aquinas insists this can't be right, for honor or glory is given to a person "on account of some excellence in him." It is a sort of flag of virtue, meant to indicate a moral, athletic, intellectual, or aesthetic accomplishment to others. Therefore, it is rightly seen as a subordinate, parasitic value, and thus could never hold the position of ultimate motivator of the will. One of the best ways to appreciate the point Aquinas is making here is to ask the simple question: Who is most honored in our society? The obvious truth that the best and most virtuous people are often least praised and the most superficial and morally questionable often the most lavishly praised gives away the game. Honor might be the icing on the cake, but it can never *be* the cake.

Still others have held that power is our ultimate good. Thomas proposes a pithy negative argument for this position. It appears that what people shun the most is servitude or incapacity; therefore, it seems to follow that what they desire the most is power. Again, especially in our Western culture, this observation finds a good deal of traction. For freedom is unquestionably our supreme cultural good, and liberty, in the final analysis, is tantamount to power, the ability to do what one wants, as one wants. J.R.R. Tolkien made the case in narrative form. We recall that the central preoccupation of the decent characters in *The Lord of the Rings* is to destroy a talisman that is identified precisely as a ring of power. To my mind, the most frightening scene in *The Lord of the Rings* has nothing to do with orcs or goblins; it is the moment when Gandalf—the great wizard, the embodiment of spiritual wisdom—spies the ring in the home of Bilbo Baggins and, for a terrible moment, is tempted to seize it for his own purposes. In accord with the adage that the corruption of the best is the worst, such a moral compromise would have been disastrous. It is instructive indeed that in Matthew's account of the temptation of Jesus by the devil, the last and most alluring suggestion of the dark spirit is that the Lord seize power: "The devil took him to a very high mountain and showed him all the kingdoms of the world and their splendor; and he said to him, 'All these I will give you, if you will fall down and worship me.'"

But despite its undoubted attractiveness, Aquinas says that power cannot be the supreme good, and this for a simple reason. Power has the nature of a principle or a source of action, whereas happiness has the nature of an end. Power, in a word, is always for something else—to move, to attain, to achieve, to acquire, etc. But, precisely as subordinate, it cannot play the role of supreme motivator of the will. A relevant observation here: power, Thomas says, can be directed to either good or evil, as we can see in a saint and a master of wickedness, both of whom wield rather enormous influence. The very ambiguity of power tells against its status as ultimate good.

Finally, many others—including some of the greatest philosophers of antiquity and modernity— have proposed that the final end of human endeavor is pleasure. This hedonistic perspective should not be construed superficially, as though the pleasure in question is crude sensual stimulation alone. Indeed, pleasure can be taken in a broad sense to include the joy that one takes in fine art, in moral accomplishment, in friendship, etc. And it does indeed appear that pleasure is that for the sake of which everything else is done. Aristotle himself said, "It is absurd to ask anyone what is his motive in wishing to be pleased." However, here again, we are dealing with a good that is parasitic upon, and derivative from, some higher and more abiding value. Thus, we feel pleasure in our bodies when we have attained some state of well-being, and we experience pleasure in our minds when we have accomplished or experienced something worthwhile. The good feeling that we have is therefore a pleasant side effect, but it should not be mistaken for the object of our deepest desiring. Moreover, we can experience pleasure from even wicked acts, which proves that good feeling in itself can never be the final, unadulterated good that the soul longs for.

Thus, neither wealth, nor pleasure, nor power, nor honor is, in point of fact, the final cause of the will's activity. So what is it? Aquinas concludes that it cannot be any worldly good, for the *beatitudo* we are talking about must be a good that utterly satisfies the appetite, and the appetite within us is for perfect goodness. Human experience reveals clearly that the attainment of even the greatest worldly goods leaves us still wanting more, still unsatisfied. C.S. Lewis observed that the insufficiency of finite goods is realized not so much at the worst moments of life, but precisely at the best, when we've tasted victory, intense pleasure, moral satisfaction, or the adulation of the crowd. For in the immediate wake of such joys, we sense that we still want more; or, to put it more positively, we sense that what we've experienced is a sort of sign or sacrament of the unconditioned good that we really and secretly desire. The hunger of the will pushes us, whether we like it or not, beyond the world. Aquinas concludes: "Hence it is evident that nothing can lull a man's will, save the universal good. This is to be found not in any creature but in God alone."

After this Thomistic excursus, let us return to the biblical story of Elijah and the priests of Ba'al. Might we construe the altars erected by the avatars of Ba'al as evocative of the various forms of false worship in which we engage? Might we imagine that there are four altars dedicated to wealth, power, pleasure, and honor? We sinners spend our lives begging, cajoling, and hopping around at these altars, imploring non-existent gods to satisfy the deepest hunger of our hearts—and this is the central tragedy of human life, the dysfunction that lies behind most of the sadness that we experience. We are wired for God, but we hook our longing for the infinite good onto some finite object that can never, even in principle, satisfy that longing.

Now, what this leads to is addiction, and it is easy to see why. We convince ourselves that we will be happy once we have enough, say, wealth and material goods. And so we strive and strive, dedicating our minds, energies, and passions to the acquiring of money. If we reach a financial goal—perhaps getting our first million by age thirty—we do indeed receive a thrill; but the thrill wears off, for we are not wired for such a finite value. We then strive more and more, working around the clock to make more money, and when we do, we feel the familiar buzz; but this time it wears off more quickly. (Talk to anyone who has been through alcohol or drug addiction, and you'll find this principle confirmed.) Now in a real panic, we give ourselves utterly to the production of wealth, hopping furiously around that particular altar. We recall that when Elijah taunted them, the priests of Ba'al commenced to slash themselves with knives until they bled. What a perfect image for the self-destruction that inevitably follows from the addictive obsession with finite values. Substitute honor, power, or pleasure for wealth, and the same dynamics obtain.

Some years ago, in the pages of *Rolling Stone* magazine, I read an interview with the actor Don Johnson. In the 1980s and 1990s, there was no more prominent figure in entertainment than Don Johnson. He was the star of the most popular television show of the era, "Miami Vice"; his sartorial taste set the tone for much of the Western world; his handsome face graced millions of magazine covers. In the course of the interview, he recalled an experience that he had had when he was at the height of his powers. He was hosting a party at his Florida estate. Revelers cavorted throughout the house, all over the grounds, and on the decks of three yachts docked in the star's private lagoon. Johnson stood on a balcony surveying the scene, and it occurred to him, at that moment, that all of his dreams of wealth, fame, power, and pleasure had come true. But instead of smiling in satisfaction, he thought, "Then why am I so [blank]ing miserable?" It was not clear from the interview what Johnson did with that insight, but it was a tremendously powerful spiritual perception and a confirmation of Lewis' intuition. It was precisely when he was in full possession of worldly goods that his heart sought—Johnson sensed painfully enough—the More.

St. John of the Cross, the greatest spiritual teacher in Western Christianity, said that we possess within ourselves infinitely deep and expansive caverns, by which he meant to suggest the longing for the infinite God. One dysfunctional strategy practiced by us sinners is to cover them over, pretending that they don't exist. We might see this at work in much of contemporary secularism, where (to shift the metaphor) the buffered self holds sway. A second classical and equally counterproductive strategy is to attempt to fill those caves with finite goods. And so we throw into the infinite abysses beautiful thing after beautiful thing, pleasure after pleasure, honor after honor, only to find that they fall uselessly into the cavernous darkness.

At this point in the analysis, we are ready to articulate the most important, though highly paradoxical, principle of spiritual physics: that the infinite God alone can satisfy the infinite hunger of the heart, and therefore, only when the soul is filled by God will it find beatitude. But who is God? According to the teaching at the very heart of Christianity,

God is love. God is self-diffusive gift. Therefore, to be filled with God is to be filled with love—which is to say, the willingness to empty oneself for the sake of the other. And so the paradox: happiness is never a function of filling oneself up; it is a function of giving oneself away. When the divine grace enters one's life (and everything we have is the result of divine grace), the task is to contrive a way to make it a gift. In a sense, the divine life—which exists only in gift form—can be "had" only on the fly. When we try to make it our own possession, it necessarily evanesces, for it can't exist in that manner. Take a good hard look at the Parable of the Prodigal Son for the details.

No one in the great tradition summed up what I've been saying over these past several pages more succinctly than St. Augustine of Hippo. On the very first page of his *Confessions*, we find the formula: "Thou hast made us for Thyself and our hearts are restless till they rest in Thee." Everything else in the psychological and spiritual life is essentially a footnote to that statement.

CHAPTER NINE

The Burning Bush

T O BRING THIS SECTION to a close, I should like to consider another deeply evocative story from the Scriptures, a passage that has proved pivotal in the spiritual and theological traditions of Christianity: Exodus chapter three, the account of Moses and the burning bush. Practically every detail of this narrative is charged with symbolic significance.

We hear that Moses, the erstwhile prince of Egypt, is now far from the courts of pharaoh, "keeping the flock" for his father-in-law Jethro on the slopes of Mt. Horeb, which rises up from the Sinai wilderness. In every spiritual tradition in the world, we can find the theme that the one who would have an experience of God must first be chastened and humbled. A self-regarding ego will never see God. Thus the impetuous and prideful Moses had to spend years in the poverty of the desert before he was ready for vision and mission. While tending his flock, Moses spies a "great sight": a bush on fire but not consumed. Retaining still some of his self-assertiveness, Moses says to himself, "I must turn aside and look at this great sight, and see why the bush is not burned up." Striding toward the strange phenomenon, Moses hears a voice: "Come no closer! Remove the sandals from your feet, for the place on which you are standing is holy ground." The true God can never be grasped, controlled, ordered by the mind, or placed in neat categories; rather, he does the controlling. I have always savored the instruction given to Moses to take off his shoes. When one is shod, one can walk easily and confidently where one wants. Removing shoes makes a person vulnerable and receptive, which is the only proper attitude in the presence of God.

The voice from the burning bush then identifies himself: "I am the God of your father, the God of Abraham, the God of Isaac, and the God of Jacob." Moses realizes he is not dealing with some impersonal absolute, but some*one*. Moreover, the God of the bush says that he has witnessed the suffering of the Hebrew people who have been enslaved in Egypt, and accordingly, he has a mission for Moses: "Come,

I will send you to Pharaoh to bring my people, the Israelites, out of Egypt." Now the visionary understands that he is dealing with a God of intelligence, will, and compassion.

After he accepts this charge (admittedly with some reluctance), Moses makes bold to ask God's name: "If I come to the Israelites and say to them, 'The God of your ancestors has sent me to you,' and they ask me, 'What is his name?' what shall I say to them?" Though it sounds innocent enough, this line of inquiry puts Moses in a very precarious spiritual space. Especially in an ancient context, to know a person's name was to establish a kind of mastery over her or him. Therefore, to pose such a question is akin to Adam and Eve's grasp at divinity in the Garden of Eden. God's answer, given in Exodus 3:14, is a *locus classicus* of Jewish and Christian theology: "I Am Who I Am. . . . Thus you shall say to the Israelites, 'I Am has sent me to you.'" In one sense, this famously cryptic response—in other translations, "He Who Is"—is no more than a tautology, perhaps a not-so-subtle way of saying, "Stop asking me such stupid questions." But the mainstream of the theological tradition has interpreted it as a strangely accurate description of God. It could be argued that Moses was asking a rather reasonable question—namely, which god are you? In his cultural context, there were gods of the mountain, of the sea, of particular places and particular people. So we might construe his question as: Which name picks you out from among this multitude of deities? But the answer that God gives does not correspond to this expectation, for he does not say that I am this deity rather than that; he says, simply enough, "I Am Who I Am." In a word, his manner of being is not specified, delimited, or categorized. Thomas Aquinas took this divine self-designation as the biblical warrant for talking about the coincidence of essence (what something is) with existence (that by which something is) in God. Whereas in every creature there is a real distinction between essence and existence—for every creature exists in a particular way or according to a definite mode—in God there is no such distinction. I am a *human* being; the keyboard on which I'm typing is an existent in a very definite manner. But to be God is, as David Burrell put it, "to be to-be."

I fully realize that this can seem to be mere theological hair-splitting, but in fact, this clarification is of great moment. One of the clearest marks of finite, worldly natures is that they exist in a mutually exclusive manner. To be a whale is not to be a tiger; to be a car is not to be a horse; to be the planet Jupiter is not to be a toaster; etc. Precisely as defined, finite things stand over and against one another. But I Am cannot be defined; he is not a being among many, not the highest instance of the genus of existing things. And it is this qualitative *difference* of God that enables him to exist noncompetitively among his creatures. The antelope could become a lion only by being devoured, by ceasing to be an antelope. A tree can become a pile of ash only by being burned up, by surrendering its unique manner of being. But the One Who Is can come close to his creatures in such a way that they are not destroyed or compromised.

Contrast this with stories in classical mythology of gods and goddesses coming close to human beings with disastrous results. The best-known narrative of this type is the myth of Semele, a young woman who served as priestess in the temple of Zeus. One day, while bathing in the river after performing a sacrifice to the father of the gods, Semele was spied by Zeus, who had assumed the form of an eagle and was circling overhead. Smitten, Zeus descended to earth in human form and began an affair with his priestess. In time, Zeus' wife Hera found out, and in her jealousy, planted seeds of doubt concerning Zeus' divinity in the mind of Semele. Eager to verify her lover's identity, Semele asked Zeus to reveal his deity to her. Though he showed but a tiny fraction of his divine perfection to her, it was enough to obliterate her and reduce her to ashes. Divinity and humanity competed for space on the same playing field, and when push came to shove, one of them had to give way. A somewhat less dramatic example of the same theme is the myth of Prometheus. Stealing the fire, which was the unique preserve of the gods, Prometheus aroused the wrath of Zeus and suffered the grim fate of having his liver chewed out and eaten daily by an eagle. In the desperate zero-sum game of classical mythology, human flourishing is an affront to the gods and must be punished.

And then there is the Bible. Let us return to the great image of the burning bush. When the true God—the God Who Is, the God whose essence is identical to his existence—comes close to creatures, they are not consumed; rather, they become more beautifully and radiantly themselves, on fire but not burned up. This theme runs through the whole Bible and was given splendid expression by St. Paul who said, in an ecstatic exclamation, "It is no longer I who live, but it is Christ who lives in me." Though his entire existence was taken over by Jesus Christ, Paul is not less himself; he is, instead, the richest version of himself. Does any reader of the Pauline literature ever sense that Paul's personality, intelligence, and distinctive character have been lost? Of course not. His unique self practically leaps off of the page. Possessed by the true God, he was more—not less—himself; he was on fire but not destroyed.

The competitive god who haunts the mind of modern people has nothing to do with the God of the Bible. There is no need for a voluntarist assertion of human will against the voluntarist god, for that deity is a bogeyman, a fantasy. St. Irenaeus of Lyon, the second-century theological master, summed up his own program—and indeed, the whole of Christianity—with the claim, "*Gloria Dei homo vivens*" ("The glory of God is a human being fully alive"). That is the manner of expression of someone who knows the God of the burning bush.

Conclusion

THE LAST TWENTY-FIVE YEARS have been bad ones for religion in general and Catholicism in particular. The clerical sexual abuse scandals, which have rocked the entire Catholic world, have amounted to a perfect storm, undermining the work of the Church in practically every way. They have led to an enormous loss of credibility in priestly leadership, a sharp decline in parish membership, and the public shaming and mockery of those who continue to express their loyalty to Catholicism. Some years ago, I appeared on a local news program in Chicago to publicize the showing of my documentary *CATHOLICISM* on public television. Here is how the interview commenced: "Father, with the possible exception of Islam, Catholicism is the most hated religion in the world. How are you going to address this problem?"

Moreover, as we saw, the events of September 11th reconfirmed in the minds of many the prejudice that religious people are fanatics, and violent ones at that. Plus, the rise in the last twenty years or so of a movement advocating for the rights of the LGBTQ community has led millions across the West to question Christianity's classical convictions regarding sexual morality. What was for so many years an unquestioned consensus now looks to many as tantamount to hate speech.

For these and other reasons, voices sharply critical of religion have sounded not only in the colleges and universities (where they have been present for some time), but also on television, the internet, and various forms of social media, where the minds of young people are shaped. In her book *iGen*, psychologist Jean Twenge has demonstrated statistically that the rising generation is by far the least religious in American history. Researchers used to pacify the faithful with the observation that, though young people were increasingly nonreligious, they remained "spiritual." This means that they weren't attending church services or subscribing to the dogmas of their faith, but they were nevertheless strong believers in God's existence, the afterlife, the power of prayer, etc. What Twenge shows unmistakably is that the current cohort of young people are increasingly both nonreligious *and* nonspiritual.

The divorce from the doctrines and practices of the classical religions has finally resulted in the withering away of the convictions that those dogmas and patterns of behavior once inculcated.

Perhaps you have been one of those vocal critics of religion. Or perhaps you are a member of the millennial or iGen generation who, surrounded by such voices, has ceased to see the need for God in your life, much less religion. Whatever your perspective on faith in the twenty-first century, remember that there is indeed a middle ground between violent imposition and bland, subjectivizing indifference—namely, the art of arguing religion. The resources of the Christian intellectual tradition—from Isaiah and Paul, to Augustine and Aquinas, to Newman, Chesterton, and John Paul II—are rich, abundant, and galvanizing. They can guide us to a faith that does not operate in a violent or browbeating manner, but still marches confidently into the public space "with fife and drum." They yield a Church that, as John Paul II put it, never imposes its point of view, but rather proposes it with creativity and intelligence. And they lead us to God, who is the answer to the deepest longing of the heart and the most ardent questing of the mind.

Although the priests of Ba'al may still outnumber the prophets of the true God, remember: only the latter cause the fire to fall.

Notes

Section One

HOW TO HAVE A RELIGIOUS ARGUMENT

---

7   **famous arguments for God's existence:**
Aquinas, *Summa theologiae* 1.2.3.

11   **"Ever since the creation of the world":**
Romans 1:20.

11   *preambula fidei* **(preambles to the faith):**
Aquinas, *Summa theologiae* 1.2.2.

11   **a *manuductio* (a leading by the hand):**
Aquinas, *Summa theologiae* 1.1.5.

12   **"by a Son":** Hebrews 1:2.

12   **"God is love, and those who abide in love abide in God, and God abides in them":**
1 John 4:16.

13   **"The kingdom of God has come near; repent, and believe (*pisteuete*) in the good news":**
Mark 1:15.

13   **"Why are you afraid? Have you still no faith (*pistis*)?":** Mark 4:40.

13   **"Go; your faith (*pistis*) has made you well":**
Mark 10:52.

13　**"Believe in God, believe also in me":**
John 14:1

14　*fides quaerens intellectum* **(faith seeking understanding):** Anselm, *Proslogion, with the Replies of Gaunilo and Anselm*, trans. Thomas Williams (Indianapolis: Hackett, 1995), 2.

14　**the claim that England is an island:** John Henry Newman, *An Essay in Aid of a Grammar of Assent* (New York: Cambridge University Press, 2010), 287.

16　**formulated by the twentieth-century Jesuit philosopher Bernard Lonergan:** Bernard Lonergan, *Method in Theology* (New York: Herder and Herder, 1972), 20.

21　**a *bios* or an entire way of life:** See Pierre Hadot, *Philosophy as a Way of Life: Spiritual Exercises from Socrates to Foucault*, ed. Arnold I. Davidson (Malden, MA: Wiley-Blackwell, 1995).

22　**the allegory of the cave:** Plato, *Republic*, trans. G.M.A. Grube, rev. by C.D.C. Reeve (Indianapolis: Hackett, 1992), 186-191.

26　**the "buffered self":** See Charles Taylor, *A Secular Age* (Cambridge, MA: Harvard University Press, 2007).

30 **"mythological world views . . . which take on legitimating functions for the occupants of positions of authority":** *Jürgen Habermas on Society and Politics: A Reader*, ed. Steven Seidman (Boston: Beacon, 1989), 134.

31 **"a veil of ignorance":** John Rawls, *A Theory of Justice* (Cambridge, MA: Harvard University Press, 1971), p. 139.

32 **"Mr. Jefferson, build up that wall!":** Talks at Google, "Christopher Hitchens | Talks at Google," YouTube video, August 16, 2007, 19:56, https://youtu.be/sD0B-X9LJjs.

35 **Second Inaugural Address:** Wikipedia's "Abraham Lincoln's second inaugural address" entry, Wikimedia Foundation, last modified April 5, 2018, 21:23, https://en.wikipedia.org/wiki/Abraham_Lincoln%27s_second_inaugural_address.

35 **The "I Have a Dream" speech:** Martin Luther King, Jr., "I Have a Dream," August 28, 1963, National Archives, https://www.archives.gov/files/press/exhibits/dream-speech.pdf.

37 **a video that went viral about a year ago:** Family Policy Institute of Washington, "Gender Identity: Can a 5'9, White Guy Be a 6'5, Chinese Woman?", YouTube video, April 13, 2016, https://youtu.be/xfO1veFs6Ho.

40 **"Religion is the opium of the masses":** Karl Marx, *Critique of Hegel's Philosophy of Right*, ed. Joseph O'Malley, trans. Annette Jolin and Joseph O'Malley (Cambridge: Cambridge University Press, 1970), 131.

40 **"God is dead, and we killed him":** Friedrich Nietzsche, *The Gay Science*, ed. Bernard Williams, trans. Josefine Nauckhoff (Cambridge: Cambridge University Press, 2001), 120.

41 **Jordan Peterson is right to point out:** Jordan Peterson, *12 Rules for Life: An Antidote to Chaos* (Toronto: Random House Canada, 2018), 192.

41 **asserting that existence precedes essence:** Jean-Paul Sartre, *Existentialism Is a Humanism*, trans. Carol Macomber (New Haven: Yale University Press, 2007), 20.

42 **"the meaning of life, of existence, and of the universe":** "THE SUPREME COURT; Excerpts From the Justices' Decision in the Pennsylvania Case," *New York Times*, June 30, 1992, https://www.nytimes.com/1992/06/30/us/the-supreme-court-excerpts-from-the-justices-decision-in-the-pennsylvania-case.html.

49 **"ultimate concern":** See Paul Tillich, *Systematic Theology* (Volume 1) (Chicago: University of Chicago Press, 1951).

53 **"Whether God exists?":** Aquinas, *Summa theologiae* 1.2.3.

54 **Thomas' devastatingly convincing formulation of the argument from evil:** Ibid.

Section Two

RELIGION AND THE OPENING UP OF THE MIND

65 **"showing the fly the way out of the fly-bottle":** Ludwig Wittgenstein, Philosophical Investigations, revised 4th ed., ed. P.M.S. Hacker and Joachim Schulte, trans. G.E.M. Anscombe, P.M.S. Hacker, and Joachim Schulte (Malden, MA: Wiley-Blackwell, 2009), 221.

67 **originally broadcast on radio:** ReasonPublic, "A Debate on the Existence of God: The Cosmological Argument -- F. C. Copleston vs. Bertrand Russell," YouTube video, March 14, 2012, https://youtu.be/hXPdpEJk78E.

68 **only as *viae* (paths or ways):** Aquinas, *Summa theologiae* 1.2.3.

74 **a video that purported to present Thomas Aquinas' cosmological argument:** Crash Course, "Aquinas and the Cosmological Arguments: Crash Course Philosophy #10,"

YouTube video, April 11, 2016, https://youtu.be/TgisehuGOyY.

76   **televised debate:** "Q&A: Religion and Atheism," Australian Broadcasting Corporation, April 9, 2012, http://www.abc.net.au/tv/qanda/txt/s3469101.htm.

83   **"every word that comes from the mouth of God":** Matthew 4:4.

84   **the story of Elijah and the priests of Ba'al:** 1 Kings 18:1-46.

86   **St. Augustine expressed the same idea:** Augustine, *The City of God*, trans. Marcus Dods, D.D. (New York: Modern Library, 2000), 516.

87   **commences with a consideration of happiness:** Aquinas, *Summa theologiae* 1-2.2.

87   **good morality is like good art:** G.K. Chesterton, "Our Note Book," *Illustrated London News*, May 5, 1928.

92   **Matthew's account of the temptation of Jesus:** Matthew 4:1-11.

94   **"It is absurd to ask anyone what is his motive in wishing to be pleased":** Quoted in Aquinas, *Summa theologiae* 1-2.2.6.

95   **"nothing can lull a man's will, save the universal good":** Aquinas, *Summa theologiae* 1-2.2.8.

98   **deep and expansive caverns:** *John of the Cross: Selected Writings*, ed. Kieran Kavanaugh, O.C.D. (Mahwah, NJ: Paulist Press, 1987), 294.

99   **the Parable of the Prodigal Son:** Luke 15:11-32.

99   **"Thou hast made us for Thyself and our hearts are restless till they rest in Thee":** Augustine, *Confessions*, trans. Frank Sheed (Indianapolis: Hackett, 1993), 3.

103   **the coincidence of essence (what something is) with existence (that by which something is) in God:** Aquinas, *Summa theologiae* 1.3.4.

103   **"to be to-be":** David B. Burrell, *Aquinas: God and Action,* 3rd ed. (Eugene: Wipf and Stock, 2016), 26.

106   **"It is no longer I who live, but it is Christ who lives in me":** Galatians 2:20.

106   **"The glory of God is a human being fully alive":** Irenaeus of Lyons, *Adversus Haereses*, 4.20.7.

110   **In her book *iGen*:** See Jean Twenge, *iGen: Why Today's Super-Connected Kids Are Growing Up*

Less Rebellious, More Tolerant, Less Happy—and Completely Unprepared for Adulthood—and What That Means for the Rest of Us (New York: Atria Books, 2017).

111 **"with fife and drum":** Wilhelm Pauck and Marion Pauck, *Paul Tillich: His Life and Thought* (Eugene: Wipf and Stock, 1976), 96.

111 **never imposes its point of view, but rather proposes it:** John Paul II, *Redemptoris Missio* (1990), no. 39.